THE SOCIOLOGICAL
STUDY OF RELIGION

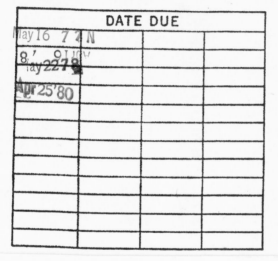

THE SOCIOLOGICAL STUDY OF RELIGION

Betty R. Scharf

*Lecturer in Sociology
in the London School of Economics*

HARPER TORCHBOOKS
Harper & Row, Publishers
New York, Evanston, San Francisco, London

This book was originally published by Hutchinson & Co. (Publishers) Ltd., London, in 1970 and is here reprinted by arrangement.

THE SOCIOLOGICAL STUDY OF RELIGION. Copyright © 1970 by Betty R. Scharf. All rights reserved. Printed in the United States of America. No part of this book may be used or reproduced in any manner without written permission except in the case of brief quotations embodied in critical articles and reviews. For information address Harper & Row, Publishers, Inc., 49 East 33rd Street, New York, N.Y. 10016.

First HARPER TORCHBOOK edition published 1971

LIBRARY OF CONGRESS CATALOG CARD NUMBER: 70-171975

STANDARD BOOK NUMBER: 06-131601-6

To my teacher
Morris Ginsberg
and to my family

CONTENTS

PREFACE

In writing this book I have had three aims in view. The first was to write a textbook which might avert for new students that panic feeling that sociology is an endless and formless subject, and that they will never be able to see the wood for the trees (or at least not within the time allowed to them for their degree courses!). I have tried to show the limits of the subject, some of the pathways into it, and some of the many points where the paths taken by different thinkers cross or merge. I have not tried to hide my preference for some paths rather than others, but I hope that the signposts on all are clear enough for the student to go ahead on his own with confidence.

My second goal was to summarise theories and approaches without committing that besetting aim of textbook sociology, the safe generalisation—safe, because fenced round with endless 'if's and but's'. It has been vividly said that Christianity is today suffering 'death by a thousand qualifications'. Textbooks also risk that fate. The jumps I have made from general to specific and back again necessarily detract from an even and systematic treatment of all topics; I hope that they help to achieve the more essential aim of keeping the reader awake.

My third purpose was to show that the sociology of religion is not only interesting in itself, but is a good approach to the basic themes of all sociology, the nature of social order, the relation of person to group, of ideas to social structure. My own conviction is that these themes are treated much more adequately via a close study of a particular aspect of human behaviour, such as the religious, than by direct attack at the most abstract and general level. I think the sociology of religion may claim to be an important and illuminating approach to these basic issues, and I have selected material in such a way as to stress this point of view.

In one important respect a purely literary treatment of the sociology of religion must be impoverished and inadequate. Religious practice in all cultures has been closely tied to the arts, to poetry and music, dance and drama, and all the visual arts. Yet this aspect of religious symbolism can hardly be brought to life by wordy description; it needs film, photograph and sound-recording. In a mere book it tends to be neglected. I think this neglect needs somehow to be remedied if we are to understand the links between religious and aesthetic experience, links which may well be vital in constructing an adequate sociology of religion.

I would like to thank my colleagues at LSE, David Martin and Percy Cohen, for stimulation and encouragement, my nephew Philip Hinchliff for helpful criticism from a student's point of view, and my secretary, Linda Walker, for her skill in converting an untidy manuscript into faultless typescript. Finally, my dedication indicates those to whom my deepest thanks are due.

I

THE SOCIOLOGICAL APPROACH TO RELIGION:
THE PIONEERS

Religious beliefs and practices have been a universal feature of human society. But not only have men prayed, worshipped and sacrificed; they have pondered deeply on their own practices, and in so doing have evolved the studies which we call theology, philosophy of religion and comparative religion. In the last hundred years, sociology—a newcomer to the world of scholarship—has staked its claim to a new way of studying religious phenomena. What is new about this claim, and how is the thought of the sociologist related to that of the philosopher or the theologian, or the student of comparative religion?

Let us start with the distinction between the theologian and the sociologist. The former begins with a faith in the divine, and tries to work out the implications of this for human life, and conversely the ways in which human experience helps us to understand the nature of divine being. Moreover, the theologian is characteristically a thinker within a particular religious tradition, Christian, Hindu, etc., concerned first with the truths, as he sees them, of that particular tradition, and only secondarily, if at all, with other religions and their relation to his own. Against this, the sociologist may be of any faith or none, and the data upon which he works may be drawn from one religious system or from many, from his own or from quite different ones. He may work within a very narrow compass, for instance the close analysis of a small and transient sect, or he may try to develop a grand theory of religion and society, and find that every kind and type of religious phenomena is grist to his mill. His job is primarily to understand the meaning for a particular society of its own religious system, and the interrelations of that religion with the social structure, and with non-religious aspects of culture, such as magic, science and technology. This attempt at sympathetic understanding may be helped or hindered by the sociologist's own personal religious position, but only in the same way as his study of any aspect of social life may be affected, for better or worse, by his special personal sympathies and knowledge. The problem of bias and values is the same here as in the other fields of social study, but in principle the sociologist of religion can, for the purpose of his study, enter into the mind of the believer without committing himself as one of the faithful. Conversely, being one of the faithful need not prevent him from standing back somewhat from his commitment when he is at work as a sociologist.

There is then a difference of intellectual posture, and a difference in the field of interest, between the theologian and the sociologist. But there is also an overlap in their interests, for if the theologian analyses human experience in order to penetrate more fully the nature of God and his actions in the world, the sociologist believes that only by analysing the particular experiences of particular societies can he make intelligible a particular set of beliefs and practices. If religion be fantasy, the particular forms of fantasy can be made intelligible only by reference to the structure and knowledge of a given society; if it be truth, then its truths are grasped and expressed according to the experience of life within a given structure and at a particular level of knowledge. Thus the work of the sociologist may contribute to that of the theologian, by exhibiting a set of beliefs in their full social context. How a set of beliefs came to be developed is a different question from their validity or consistency; on this latter aspect of the theologian's work the sociologist falls silent.

The philosopher of religion shares this latter task with the theologian, though often without the specific commitment of the latter. As metaphysician, he argues for and against the existence of God; as epistemologist, he is concerned with the meaning of the claim that men can know God, whether by revelation, by natural theology, or in other ways. Finally, as ethical theorist, he is concerned with the relations between religion and morality. In this last aspect he is often interested in those analyses of religion and social structure which are the prime task of the sociologist, but he may also tangle with the sociologist in his capacity as epistemologist, since many sociological theories of religion come up against the question of what kinds of knowledge man can attain to, and in what ways. While the sociologist may stimulate the moral theorist by presenting new, or newly organised, data on social values and norms, the sociologist may also be stimulated by the philosopher to realise more fully what theory of knowledge his work implies. Thus positivist sociologists working in the realm of religion have been criticised for assuming that methods of study suited to the world of natural objects are also adequate for the study of symbolic systems, such as religion or magic.

The next body of work whose relation to religious sociology should be assessed is that of comparative religion. This has a venerable tradition, and in fact cannot, in older or newer forms, be sharply marked off from the sociology of religion. The difference is one of focus; on the one hand, on the content of particular beliefs, rites or codes of ethics, and on the other, on the place of these beliefs, rites and codes in the context of particular social structures. The sociologist believes that while a listing or comparison of elements is extremely useful, particularly in showing up the generality or frequency of certain themes, there are further gains in understanding to be made by seeing them always in their social context.

I have tried to make these distinctions sharply in order to show what is new in the sociological approach. Of course, not every thinker fits exactly into one category or the other, and many writers, long before the name of 'sociology' was coined in the mid-nineteenth century by Comte, in fact were interested in the relations between religion and society. From our own history, one might quote Hooker's famous apologia for the Anglican church, *The Laws of Ecclesiastical Polity*; from Islam, the cyclical theory of religious and political change developed by Ib'n Khaldun. The novelty of the sociology of religion was rather that questions which had been secondary or peripheral now became the central focus of interest, and at the same time there developed this attitude of detachment, often coupled, in the earlier writers, with a personal rejection of any religious faith.

Comte gave sociology its name, impetus and direction, and stamped it from the beginning with his positivist philosophy. This can be seen very clearly in the sociology of religion. Positivists believed that social facts could be treated as things, that investigators of those things could adopt a position of complete objectivity in relation to them, and that investigations undertaken from this standpoint would gradually build up a body of empirical generalisations from which the laws of society could be derived. These laws would be of two kinds: statements of the necessary coexistence of certain social facts, that is laws of social statics, and statements of necessary sequences, or laws of social dynamics. Comte's famous law of the three stages[1] combined static and dynamic statements: the first, or theological, stage of thought was coupled with military and hierarchical social organisation; the second, or metaphysical, stage of thought with democratic and egalitarian social organisation; and the third, or positive, stage of thought would be coupled with the rule of sociologically educated experts. The three types of thought necessarily followed one another, each correcting the faults of an earlier stage. Positivists believed that this construction of a science of society could go ahead once men had ceased to ask unanswerable questions of the ultimate meaning or purpose or origin of life, and confined themselves to seeking answers to the proper 'scientific' questions of how observable things worked. The natural sciences had forged ahead once they were divorced from religious and metaphysical considerations; sociology could do the same, once this liberation was achieved.

It is easy to see how this attitude, especially when combined with personal agnosticism, tended to produce theories of religion which explained it as some kind of collective delusion, or as a kind of symbolic thinking and acting whose meaning had been somehow forgotten or misunderstood. Thus we get within the positivist tradition theories such as those of Spencer, Tylor, Frazer and Durkheim, which all begin from the assumption that men do not, in their religion, apprehend a reality outside themselves, but rather come to imagine, because of certain mysterious aspects of human existence, spirits, gods and supernatural forces. Their thinking is immature, uncontrolled by pragmatic tests, and perhaps goes awry under the influence of powerful emotions.

Positivism also encouraged a concentration on theories of social evolution. The successful application of evolutionary ideas in geology and biology during the nineteenth century no doubt was one reason for this, but another influence was probably the growing mass of material which was becoming available as exploration, trade, imperial government and Christian missions spread over the globe. Whereas previously the students of comparative religion had compared with one another the scriptural religions of literate peoples, now the sociologist could also learn about a vast variety of preliterate peoples in Africa, the Americas, Asia, Oceania and Australasia. It was not Islam, Buddhism or Hinduism that fascinated, so much as this overwhelming new mass of facts about a vast variety of small-scale, technologically primitive peoples. It cried out for classification and comparison, and scholars hoped that because of its very abundance of instances it would lend itself to generalisation. If the religions

of these many diverse and separate peoples could be accurately described and classified, and their social structure and technology likewise, surely it would be possible to show what kinds of religion were correlated with each kind of structure or technology. And as technology could be assumed to be a progressive factor in human development, farming superseding hunting, and specialisation and trade superseding isolated self-sufficiency, surely it would be reasonable to see modern preliterate societies as the representatives of the truly primitive or first state of human society.[3] Archaeology and ancient history would provide evidence of the next stages of social evolution, the ancient civilisations of the Middle East and China. The latest of these, the Graeco–Roman, was envisaged as the next step, and from there the continuity with modern European civilisation was obvious. In this fashion, though with considerable refinements in the classification of the modern 'primitive' peoples, the line of social development was conceived. Once all known societies had been ordered into this sequence, the trend in their scale and internal organisation could be discerned. It was, in Spencer's classic formulation, a movement from simple small-scale homogeneity to complex large-scale heterogeneity. There seemed a fairly straightforward parallel in the religious field, from animism, i.e., the worship of many different spirits and sacred powers, among primitives, through a polytheistic stage to be found in the ancient civilisations, to a full-blown monotheism which had developed in recent times from seeds sown during the period of early civilisation. The controversies within this general scheme were over such questions as the generality of totemism, and whether it was the most primitive form of religion. A second was over the relation of religion to magic, and of the latter to proto-science, and a third was concerned with the possibility that the earliest stage in the evolutionary sequence was one of animatism, i.e., a belief in impersonal sacred forces rather than personified spirits.

This last argument was not just a matter of difficulty in interpreting the often sketchy information about very simple hunting and gathering peoples. It became tangled with speculations on how belief in spirits and powers and magical techniques could come into existence. How had all these mistakes and illusions taken hold? Broadly speaking, two lines of argument were put forward. One, initiated by Spencer, pointed to all these phenomena of death, dreams, sleep and trances, which were likely to give rise to the idea of a soul separable from the body which it animated. The temporary separation of the soul from the body during sleep explained the

phenomena of dreams; death was a permanent departure of the soul
for some other haunt. The souls or ghosts of the dead would be
propitiated, just as living men received the respect due to their
position. Equally they might be cajoled or coaxed, or their favours
sought by making gifts to them. Thus the *do ut des* of sacrifice
would develop. Further, by analogy the non-human parts of the
environment, especially those possessed of movement and power,
such as the sun, rain, rivers, storms, would also be deemed to have
indwelling spirits, to become the haunts of human ghosts. These
spirits, particularly where the objects in question affected human
welfare, would similarly be propitiated and worshipped. On this
theory, which Tylor largely shared, the origins of religion were to be
found in man's intellectual curiosity, in his capacity to see analogies
and to generalise from them. His first religious belief would be in
personal spirits, not in impersonal powers, because the prototype
would be the life-giving principle of the human person, his soul.
But these beliefs would be subject to testing by further human
experience, on a rough trial-and-error basis. Thus it would gradually
seem more intellectually satisfying to postulate a few major deities
each in charge of a large range of phenomena or the fate of a whole
group, and still later to imagine one divine power ruling a universe
created to his design and with an almost completely orderly structure
which men could learn to understand.

J. G. Frazer's[2] variant of this intellectualist theory of religion was
to postulate a stage of magic existing before any kind of religion
developed, and being gradually overlaid rather than extinguished
by subsequent religious beliefs. Frazer argued that men's first
arguments by analogy would lead them to believe two propositions,
that what is done to the part will have an analogous effect on the
whole, and that what is done to an object will affect other objects
with which it normally comes into contact. These beliefs in homeo-
pathic and contagious magic are evidence of intelligence, not of
stupidity, evidence of the continuing effort by man to control his
world. Actions based on these beliefs may often seem to confirm
them; but gradually counter-evidence will accumulate and men will
see that they do not in fact control events by these magical practices.
In searching for another means of control, they turn to the analogy
with human conduct, the necessity for the weak to supplicate the
strong. What magic will not force nature to concede, religious
supplication may induce her to give. On this theory, the first religious
objects are not necessarily personal; it is their power which is their
essential characteristic. Frazer concedes the transformation of

religion towards a more monotheistic viewpoint, but argues that these transformations are often only accomplished by a limited educated or literate class; the tendency of the masses was to persist in or revert to the faulty generalisations of magic. (Here his view coincides with that of Weber, who from a different starting-point also argued that in all societies the 'common man' found satisfaction in magic.) Frazer also accepted the view that the advance of science was a powerful means, first to the refinement of religious doctrines and secondly to their decline and extinction.

The second line of argument about the origin of religion and magic stressed, not intellectual curiosity and beliefs, but rather emotion and ritual. Put yourself in the position of primitive man, said these theorists, and imagine yourself surrounded by forces of nature upon which you depend for your survival, but which you do not know how to control. Some important regularities are clear to you: the rhythm of day and night; the march of the seasons; the habits of game animals; the regular ripening of the crops. But there are inexplicable contingencies which may arouse intense fear; the crops may be scanty, the rains late, or the women barren. Emotion thus aroused in all breasts simultaneously demands an outlet. Great hopes and great fears must express themselves in action; as the action is collective it gradually becomes stereotyped into a ritual, and then it serves not so much to express an intense anxiety but to forestall the mounting of fear and anxiety in conditions where success in an activity is vital, yet the means to success are not all within man's control. Man, of all the animals, is the only worrier, and that explains why he is also the only animal practising religion. Ritual is the primary fact of religion, for through it men's fears are allayed or forestalled, and confidence regained; the rites are then explained by myths, creeds or dogmas concerning spirits, forces, gods and demons, but this explanation is secondary in time and importance. Men will together enact a rite, and feel its enactment as supremely important. Their explanation of why they do it will be confused and even contradictory. The rite is vital, the explanations are, so to speak, optional.

I have put these two lines of approach as contrasts to one another, and this is largely how they appeared in the history of thought, but it is apparent that they can complement one another. Those who follow the intellectualist line admitted that the belief in ghosts and spirits was a belief tinged always with the emotion of fear or awe. Why should this be so, if their postulation was just a matter of solving an intellectual puzzle about dreams and trances? Why should belief in spirits or spells bringing luck or success in fundamental matters of human life—fertility, food supply, group solidarity, etc.—be so persistent in the face of failure, unless they were the result of strong and ineradicable human emotions? On the other hand, the fact that even if ritual is the more important, no people is without its equipment of explanatory myth or belief, and that these vary not in a quite arbitrary fashion, but with some tendencies towards linkage and systematisation, suggests that we must remember that man is not only the only worrier; he is also the only animal with language as the tool of speculative thought as well as practical effort.

In order to make any sense of the view that religion has evolved from magic and animism to polytheism, then to monotheism or pantheism, it is necessary to recognise both intellectual and emotional elements in man's make-up. More important still, it is necessary to have a theory of their interconnection. Two men, both in their way inheritors and critics of the positivist tradition, attempted just such a theory; they were Durkheim and Hobhouse. But before turning to their work, I would like to mention one attempt to criticise the positive evolutionists during the heyday of their intellectual esteem. I refer to the work of Father Schmidt[3] and his colleagues in Austria. They also were very interested in all the accumulating evidence about primitive religion, and they also shared the view that modern primitives could be taken as representatives of the true prehistorical primitive human societies. Schmidt noticed that as well as numerous spirits, gods and godlings in each of these religions, there was also a great God, or high God, who very often was the central figure of a creation myth, and the guarantor of the continuing natural and social order. He was more a figure of myth than a centre of cult; devotion or sacrifice was offered to the lesser spirits rather than the high God. Schmidt argued from this coexistence of belief in a high God and in many godlings a case for primitive monotheism. He thought that regardless of technology, scale or contact with other peoples, all men had some glimmerings of the true nature of God, but that these tended to be overlaid or contaminated by animistic practices. Monotheism, then, was a matter of direct apprehension of divine reality, possibly direct revelation by God of his own nature, and not the product, as the positivists would have it, of a long and often interrupted intellectual pilgrimage. Schmidt's ideas had little influence outside European Catholic circles, but I mention them to show how the union of positivist, agnostic and evolutionary points of view was not universal in the nineteenth-century sociology of religion; Schmidt believed with the others in the practicability of

the search for evolutionary sequences, but the stages of religion he identified were quite different from theirs.

Hobhouse's contribution to the sociology of religion was part of his search for the principles of social evolution, in which he did not repudiate Spencer's account so much as supplement it, and try to explain the failures and setbacks as well as the advances on the road to greater differentiation and organisation. He argued that the movement from simple to complex could be analysed into four different movements: an expansion of scale, an increase in efficiency, an increase in mutuality or cooperation between the interdependent members of society, and an increase in the freedom of those members to choose their roles in the differentiated and interdependent whole. Advances in scale and efficiency generally went hand in hand, but the impact of these changes was often to limit the freedom and willingness to cooperate of the members. Up to a point cooperation could be enforced, but the greater the degree of coercion the greater the risk of rebellion or apathy, both of which would hinder further advances in scale and efficiency. Thus social development was chequered, not progressive; experiments in defining common goals and achieving freedom in larger and more technologically advanced societies were constantly being made, and as frequently coming to grief. Yet he could not doubt that man would return again and again to the task, for it was of his essence that he should seek to achieve in society that harmony and consistency of activity that he strove for in his individual life. Or rather, since all men are social beings, they cannot achieve harmony in their own lives unless their societies are harmonious, and if two societies are in contact, then that contact must be harmonious if it is not to frustrate the strivings of members of one or both of the societies. But while the pattern of human action in constructing the 'City of God' was 'two steps forward and one step back', the capacity of man for intellectual activity is not closely tied to practical action. He can imagine, theorise and speculate, not without any reference to experience, but not in close correspondence with it. Intellectual development, whether manifested in art, science, ethics, philosophy or religion, has a degree of freedom from social structure. Thus Hobhouse saw the movement from animism to polytheism to monotheism, and the accompanying movement to construct a universal ethical ideal of conduct, as but one aspect of the growth of mind whose 'generic function', he argued, was 'to establish articulate connections between the scattered portions of experience, and so enable its possessors to learn from the past how to provide for the future'.[4] But though the test of the religious or

ethical ideal may be how 'it provides for the future', there are great
difficulties in the application of this test in any conclusive way. In
order to 'establish articulate connections between the scattered
portions of experience', mental effort in philosophy or theology will
generally arrive at some construct of a transcendental god or ultimate
ground of being, so abstract that no empirical evidence suffices to
establish or refute its existence. Ethical ideals, for a rather different
reason, are equally difficult of confirmation or refutation by experience; this is summed up in the well-known saying 'It's not that
Christianity has been tried and found wanting, it is that it hasn't
been tried'. Put in other words, no large group has lived for long by
an ethic of unqualified love, and we cannot therefore know how
practicable or satisfying this would be. The sceptics would answer
that the very fact that experiments in such forms of living are so
few and so short-lived prove that they are impracticable and unsatis-
fying, given man's instinctive equipment. Hobhouse comes down on
this latter side of the argument, and discerns a movement in ethics
away from God-given absolutes and ascetic imperatives towards a
morality of disciplined fulfilment in which all rules lie continually
under the question, what are their consequences in human happiness?
From the point of view of religious beliefs he sees a movement
towards emphasising the common elements of all monotheistic
beliefs, and towards recognition of the essential and ineradicable
paradox of the God both all-good and all-powerful. He expects
these lessons from experience to lead to a view that God is a name
for the creative power of mind in matter, which is both love and
understanding. He diverges from his positivist predecessors in trying
to work out a view of human mind in which reason or intelligence
is not a separate faculty from instincts and emotions, but the name
of that effort towards a unity of thought, feeling and experience
which man carries further forward than any other animal. Religion
among primitive peoples may derive chiefly from emotions of fear,
anxiety and elation, but is not reducible to a simple expression of
emotion. Neither will it die out when, through greater control of his
environment, man has reduced the occasions evoking such strong
emotions. Such control makes possible a more critical and reflective
attitude to experience, one of whose fruits is the whole body of
religious and ethical thought. Religion, so far as it has always
emphasised order against chaos, obligation against impulse, has
expressed a truth of human experience, not mere fantasy and illusion.
Its origins in primitive conditions of life do not explain the forms it
has developed in quite different conditions; thus Hobhouse, though

an admirer of the Comtean tradition of positivist and evolutionary thought, retains a sympathy with the idealist philosophy which leads him to rather different conclusions from the positivists. At the philosophical level he grants a truth to religious formulations which many of the positivists deny; at the purely sociological level, he tackles the problem of the relation of religion, morality and social structures with more awareness of its complexities, and without expecting to find simple correlations between types of religion and types of society. Though his way of thinking has had few successors among sociologists, it has obvious affinities with some who have come to the philosophy and sociology of religion by way of biological studies, as, for instance, Julian Huxley, Alister Hardy and Teilhard de Chardin.

The other thinker who both continued and altered the positivist and evolutionist school was Emile Durkheim, roughly Hobhouse's contemporary. His influence is still strong, even though much of his work has been demolished by criticism. He sought, like earlier evolutionists, to find the origins of religion by analysing the religion of the supposedly most primitive society, believing that the subsequent changes in form would not radically alter its nature. He too believed that a grading of known societies from simple to complex would represent the course of social evolution, and he believed also that religion could be studied in a new way by the sociologist, as a social fact, as a thing. Yet he was unimpressed by the explaining away of religion as the product of false reasoning or mere fantasy under emotional stress; for how, he asked, could mere fantasy or illusion have such continuing and universal power in all human societies? Religion must be in some sense true in order to have such social effectiveness. In examining Durkheim's theory, it is well to remember that it is axiomatic for his sociology that the rules and values of a given society exist for its members as something above and beyond them. Each member feels them as having an existence independent of, and more enduring than, his own, and as having the power to constrain and yet uphold him. He feels his dependence on society. But religion is the acknowledgement of dependence on a superior power, the acknowledgement being made in rituals which enable the worshipper to put himself in the right relationship to this power, to receive benefits and avoid injuries from it. Is this analogy between the relationship of the individual to society, and of individual worshipper to sacred things only an analogy? Durkheim thinks not, and works confidently to the conclusion that the sacred things of any religious system are in fact symbols of the society practising that religion. What causes this felt dependence on society to be expressed in religious rituals? Durkheim develops the argument that since people having only a very primitive hunting and gathering technology must of necessity live most of their lives scattered over a wide area in tiny groups, the rare occasions on which they do come together in large numbers generate such a strong current of sociability that some collective expression of this feeling develops. Repeated on successive occasions it becomes stereotyped into a ritual, and whatever objects provide the focus of the ritual are endowed in the minds of the participants with sacred power. The emotion expressed by the ritual is projected on to objects which thereby become sacred for that group and capable of evoking the emotions of religious awe in face of a mysterious power.

The example by which he developed this argument was the Arunta tribe of central Australia, whose chief cult was of the clan totem, but where there were also lesser cults of tribal and personal totems, and also a belief, lacking cultic expression, in a supreme creator spirit. Durkheim argued that the less important tribal cult represented the lesser importance of tribe membership, as compared with clan membership, for the individual Arunta; it was clan membership that counted in most occasions of social life. The personal totem represented the internalisation of social values, the recognition that individuality depends for its creation and support on society, that each depends on all. The belief in a high God represents the dim awareness that all men are linked together, but there are so few occasions on which this perception is reinforced by experience that no cultic expression develops. Durkheim chose the Arunta as a test case for his ingenious argument, but this very case appears to refute it, since the important clan totemic rites are performed at assemblies convened especially for that purpose, while other occasions for assembly are not associated with religious rites. To make facts begin to fit his thesis one would have to assume that the totemic assemblies had first been held for other purposes, that the rituals then grew as a by-product of the other activities, and that finally the latter dropped out, or were displaced to other occasions. But even this line of argument, which is weak because untestable, cannot deal with the fact that there are regular assemblies of large numbers of tribesmen at which no religious rituals are performed. If crowd emotion is the essential raw material of religion, then a crowd regularly gathered for whatever purpose should generate ritual and symbol. Finally there is the difficulty that the groups that gather for ritual are differently composed from those which gather for other activities; it seems to be not just numbers, but types of group, which generate ritual. All these weaknesses are specific to Durkheim's theory; in addition, there is one which it shares together with earlier versions of evolutionary theory, the view that to understand the nature of religion among primitives, to understand its origins, is to understand its essence at all times and in all types of society.

These criticisms all concern Durkheim's speculations on the cause of religion; but true to his own rule of sociological method, he also offers an explanation of its function. To this I now turn, noting on the way that the accounts of origin lead to the conclusion that a given social group generates a morality and a religion to express and symbolise it. A religion is specific to a group, and where one group ends and another begins religion changes. From the point of view of origins, group structure is primary and religion is the dependent variable. But from the functional point of view Durkheim sees religion as powerfully reinforcing a given social structure, restraining deviance and limiting change by giving an absolute and sacred authority to the group's existing rules and values. Religion thus both derives from social solidarity and in its turn strengthens it. It both expresses group loyalties and continues them. But though religion may impede change it cannot totally inhibit it. The conditions of a group's existence change, and the structure changes in response. Whether explicitly or covertly, suddenly or gradually, the religious system changes, though always fighting rearguard actions. There is always some group which is sacred to its members, therefore though religions change and develop, no society can fail to generate a religion, and no religion can fail to strengthen its specific society. Like Hobhouse, Durkheim accepted that with the growth of societies in scale and mutual contacts, with the growth of science and technology, men would move forward in thought from clan totems, ancestor spirits and tribal or city gods, to the conception of one God ruling all creation. But the experience which fuelled religious feeling would still be the experience of living in a particular group with its own particular traditions, rules and values. Thus the monotheistic religions would tend to combine a theoretic universalism with a practical commitment to the defence and reinforcement of particular groups; the God of all mankind would be invoked to justify the special position of a particular people. Alternatively, the monotheistic God might be in a position similar to that of the Arunta high God, believed in but not worshipped because the effective 'sacred thing' was the national flag, or the political leader. The truth or reality of religion, as Durkheim saw it, was its efficacy in promoting confidence and conformity among members of a particular group; sociological explanation lay in the detailed analysis of how particular social structures gave rise to, and were reflected in, particular religious systems.

Durkheim's theory of religion is usually taken to be fully expounded in his book *The Elementary Forms of Religious Life*.[5] But it is worth while also considering the relevance of the main thesis of his earlier work, *Division of Labour*.[6] This book shows Durkheim to be fully in the evolutionary tradition, much more so than in *Elementary Forms*, which gives an analysis of one primitive religion in great detail, but only a very brief, if suggestive, account of the social concomitants of the development towards monotheism and universalism. Like Hobhouse, Durkheim plays his own variation on the Spencerian theme of evolution from simple homogeneous societies to complex highly organised heterogeneous ones. The theme of the *Division of Labour* is that human societies have progressively changed from a simple horde-like type, in which there is no differentiation of role apart from that dictated by age and sex, to a very complex type in which a very great number and variety of specialised tasks are performed by different members of the society. The first type of society is characterised by 'mechanical solidarity', members sharing the same knowledge and experience and therefore accepting the same rules, values and authority. In such a society, any breach of the rules will be treated as an attack on the whole, as a kind of treason or sacrilege. 'Mechanical solidarity' is that which is upheld by the 'sacred things' of the society. Durkheim speculated that the initial move to specialisation and division of labour took place under conditions of population pressure, when 'mechanical solidarity' was so strong that alternative responses of fleeing or fighting were inhibited. Once some degree of differentiation had taken place, the process developed its own momentum. More choices of way of life were available and this sharpened and developed individuality; people were no longer so alike in their experience, and therefore in the authorities and the values they accepted. As standards of living rose, so new needs came over the horizon. The number of rules whose breach was treason or sacrilege diminished, yet others multiplied to regulate the multifarious relations of specialised jobs and social positions. But these latter did not attain the same status as the old kind of rule; they formed a body of restitutive law, recognising the network of obligations between different social positions, and providing that anyone who failed in such a duty should be liable to compensate the person to whom it was due. The older rules comprised repressive law, where society as a whole demanded expiation or exacted retribution, because the collective consciousness and solidarity of the whole was felt to be injured by the crime. Clearly, restitutive law is concerned with profane, not sacred, things; and in a society with a large body of such rules, i.e., where division of labour has proceeded far, 'mechanical solidarity' is residual; it is nevertheless extremely important in Durkheim's view because it is on this basis of likeness, of shared values and symbols, that differentiation can develop without issuing in disruption. Durkheim also argues that a society with highly developed division of labour will, or at least may, develop a sense of organic solidarity, a recognition of the complementarity and interdependence of parts. In his treatment of the conflicts and anomie (failure to accept social obligations or norms) observable in the rapidly industrialising Europe of his day, he is fairly optimistic that in each nation this organic solidarity would grow and internal conflicts diminish. Even so, this organic solidarity cannot, by Durkheim's own account, be symbolised in sacred things, as the mechanical solidarity of simple societies could be, because the individual is not simply under the power of a single and apparently unchanging set of rules and values, but knows himself to have a measure of choice and freedom in selecting his roles in society. In making this choice he is aware of change and variety, and even inconsistency of social rules. Moreover there will be many sub-groups to which he may give some of his loyalty. The function of religion, Durkheim thought, was to retard social change and maintain the solidarity of existing groups, and in his *Elementary Forms* he argues that so far as a particular religion cannot perform this function successfully, new groups will arise which in their turn will become sacred to their members. So far as modern industrial societies are concerned he saw Nationalism and Communism as successor religions to the various forms of Christianity, arguing that no society can live which does not give to its members a vision of an ideal form of life and a ritual expression of this ideal. Yet in his *Division of Labour* he develops a theory of the relation of individuals, sub-groups and society which suggests strongly that modern industrial societies must be more secular, and will have not merely different religions, but less compelling ones.

I believe that in *Division of Labour* is to be found a more adequate causal account of religion than in the much criticised speculative history of the *Elementary Forms*. However, an attempt to combine the approaches of both works does throw up some difficulties, and apparent inconsistencies, as suggested in the previous paragraph. It may be argued that both Durkheim's conclusions have been proved right in respect of modern industrial societies, i.e., that sometimes Nationalism or Communism have developed with religious fervour and appropriate rituals, and sometimes there has been a clear advance of secularisation. While this is true, the difficulty remains that Durkheim's different accounts do not allow him to specify which social or psychological factors are responsible for the different situations of old faith, new faith or no faith. The sociologist's task of trying to find these factors still remains.

Despite the weaknesses of Durkheim's theory, particularly in its handling of anthropological evidence, its functional analysis has had enormous influence, especially in social anthropology. In Durkheim's lifetime his pupils, Hubert and Mauss,[7] applied it to Eskimo social structure and religious activities, trying to show the same rhythm of concentrated and dispersed social life, linked with much and little ritual activity, which Durkheim thought he had discerned among the Arunta. Since then a great deal of effort has been, and is still being, expended by social anthropologists in making functional analyses of primitive religion. At first, they were concerned only with religions which were basically communal or tribal, where religious participation was an aspect of group membership, and where it seemed reasonable to assume a stable and rather isolated social structure. Later they developed a great interest in the sudden changes in religion which appeared when the disruptive influences of European trade and settlement were felt by primitive peoples. Work in respect of both the relatively stable and isolated, and the rapidly changing preliterate societies, is continuing, though naturally the emphasis is now more on the latter type of society, as more and more peoples are brought within the influence of trade, travel, literacy and foreign government.

In summarising the development of the sociology of religion, it is necessary to comment also on some contributors who stand outside the positivist, evolutionary tradition which used to dominate the subject. Marx, Troeltsch and Max Weber have given to the study of religion in complex societies the same sort of stimulus which Durkheim gave to its study in simpler ones.

Marx was an evolutionist, in matters religious as well as economic, but for him the movement towards social complexity was also and always a movement towards social conflict, the conflict of economic interest groups or classes. Though he was prepared to generalise about religion in all societies, he was chiefly interested in religion in class-ridden societies, and in the role of religion in expressing or hindering the growth of class consciousness among the exploited. Marx it was who summed up his ideas in the famous sentences: 'Religion is the moan of the oppressed creature, the heart of a heartless world, the sense of seneless conditions. It is the opium of the people.'[8]

But it was Engels who did most of the detailed studies, trying to relate specific religious phenomena to the class divisions of particular societies. For instance, he tried to explain the early spread of Christianity in terms of the growth of a proletariat, both slave and free, in the towns of the Graeco–Roman empire. He analysed the sixteenth-century German Peasants' War, in which the peasants used religious symbols and followed a religious leader, as part of the dying throes of feudalism. Both men emphasised that religion could be a mode of protest as well as of acceptance or resignation, and tried to identify the conditions under which class conflicts were either expressed or denied in religious terms. This led them, Engels in particular, to study Christian sectarianism, a field in which Troeltsch and Weber also did great pioneer work.

Troeltsch was a German historian of a generalising turn of mind. As a Christian and as a scholar he was interested in the diversity of groups with Christendom, particularly in Western Christianity. In his great survey of Christian history up to the eighteenth century, entitled *The Social Teachings of the Christian Churches*,[9] he worked out a typology of church, sect and mystic group, which has proved to be of great interest to all sociologists of religion since his day. Weber's studies of sects derive directly from Troeltsch, and among other writers who express their debt to him are Bryan Wilson in England and H. R. Niebuhr in the USA. Troeltsch believed in the importance of the original gospel of Christianity in influencing all subsequent developments. Taking this gospel, with its basic beliefs in the incarnation and resurrection of Christ and the final judgement of God, as given, he attempts to show how believers in different social positions, cultured or uncultured, deprived or privileged, uprooted or stable, will tend to emphasise one aspect of the gospel at the expense of the rest. Thus alongside the church which has to compromise with a world of sinners there will occur recurrently the twofold protest of the sectarian who attempts and demands moral and religious perfection on this earth, and the mystic for whom sacraments, organisation and moral rules are all unimportant compared with the individually achieved communion with God. In his basic ideas, Troeltsch was poles apart from Marx and Engels, yet he agreed with them that sectarian outbursts were correlated with low social position. For him, however, injustice and inequality were permanent aspects of the fallen condition of man, so that the tension of church, sect and mystic would continue so long as Christianity lasted; he did not predict, as did Marx, that the religious protest of the sect would be transformed into the more effective political protest of the party, and eventually herald a revolution which would do away with all injustice (and of course with Christianity also!). Troeltsch limited his typology to Christian societies before the age of rapid industrialisation, but his successors have tried to apply it to Christian groups in industrialising societies, and to consider its applicability in other than Christian settings.

Thus Max Weber, who was also very interested in sects, thought of them not as necessarily deriving in part from the basic Christian gospel, but rather as a sub-type of a more general category of 'other worldly' religion, contrasted with 'this worldly' religion, into which Troeltsch's category of churches would fall. Weber, like Marx, worked on a wider basis than Troeltsch, but, unlike Marx, made religion one of his central sociological interests. He took immense pains to study and write on all the major religions of the world, considered in their detailed historical and sociological setting. The scale of his work has not been matched by any other writer; except for Islam he has published works on all the major religions of the world.[10] Apart from his debt to Troeltsch and his reaction against Marx, he appears as a pioneer following quite different paths from those of the evolutionists and the positivists. He was more interested in the differences than in the similarities of religious systems, and though he offers a few statements on the general direction of social change, he has no theory of social evolution. Like Marx, his major interest was in the development of Western capitalism, but unlike Marx he did not view it as a stage in the universal history of society, but rather as an historically unique phenomenon. Why it had not developed elsewhere was Weber's problem, and he sought the answer in the different economic ethics of the world religions. He thought that the kind of economic ethics favourable to capitalist enterprise was only to be found in Protestant Christianity, and to a lesser extent in Judaism. To establish this conclusion he needed to carry out a vast work of classification, and in doing this he developed a number of concepts which all writers since his day have found extremely useful. A fuller discussion of them follows in Chapter 7. Most of his work has been published posthumously from unfinished manuscripts and lecture notes, and thus gives the impression of work in progress rather than a completed opus. But despite, or perhaps because of this, his influence on the sociology of religion has been immense, greater even than that of Durkheim.

Coming to sociology from the German academic tradition, rather than from Anglo-Saxon Positivism, Weber was always convinced that social studies required a different method from natural sciences. The social investigator had not merely to observe from outside, but to understand the meaning of social actions to the actors. In stressing the need to understand purposes and meanings, Weber is in line with the modern anthropological students of religion, and in contrast to earlier theorists who imputed, particularly to primitive peoples, various kinds of illusory or illogical thinking because this was how it appeared to the outside observer. Weber shared the positivists' ambitions no more than their method. He thought that the complexity of historical data and the inevitable involvement of the investigator with his subject-matter together ensured that there could not be a gradual building up of an edifice of sociology, brick by brick, study by study. All historical and sociological investigation involved a selection from the immense totality of human actions, a selection made according to the interests and values of the investigator. Different students would therefore arrive at different and partial truths, and there could never be any final or complete achievement of truth in respect of human societies. Thus he makes no overwhelming claims for his sociology of religion. Through it he attempts to show the power of ideas in social change, but his approach is undogmatic and unpolemical. This again may be one of the reasons for his wide appeal.

To complete this summary of the pioneers I would mention the work of Le Bras[11] in France. He began his work under Durkheim's influence, but it bore its own distinctive stamp. He was interested primarily in what might be called the sociography of religion, the detailed plotting of the extent of religious practice and affiliation, particularly in contemporary France and in recent French history. Through the studies that he carried out and stimulated among his pupils, a very complete picture of the strengths and weaknesses of French Catholicism has been built up. Le Bras, though a Catholic, was primarily an academic. Some of his successors have been interested in the practical tasks of strengthening the church in France, for which an understanding of the reasons for its weaknesses is requisite. Studies similar to Le Bras' have been carried out in the USA, Latin America, and many European countries. With the growth of survey methods, there has been a great development of studies in church attendance, degree of religious belonging and involvement, and of belief and knowledge of religious dogmas. Survey methods have been criticised for superficiality and ambiguity of answers, but they have, within their limitations, provided enough information to show, for instance, that the question of the relations between industry, town life, social class, and religious practice is a very complex one. In the last chapter some of this information, and its bearing on theories of religion, will be discussed.

1. A. Comte, *The Positive Philosophy*, trans. and condensed by H. Martineau, 1853.

2. J. G. Frazer, *Magic and Religion*, ch. IV, 1944.

3. W. Schmidt, *The Origin and Growth of Religion*, 1931.

4. L. T. Hobhouse, *Morals in Evolution*, 7th ed., 1951, pp. 384–6.

5. E. Durkheim, *The Elementary Forms of Religious Life*, trans. by J. W. Swain, 1915.

6. E. Durkheim, *The Division of Labour in Society*, trans. by G. Simpson, 1947.

7. M. Mauss, 'Essai sur les Variations Saisonnières des Sociétés Eskimos', *Année Sociologique*, vol. IX.

8. K. Marx, 'Critique of the Hegelian Philosophy of Law', in *Economic and Philosophical Manuscripts*, 1844.

9. E. Troeltsch, *The Social Teachings of the Christian Churches*, trans. by O. Wyon, 1931.

10. M. Weber, *Sociology of Religion*, trans. by E. Fischoff, 1965.
—*The Protestant Ethic and the Spirit of Capitalism*, trans. by T. Parsons, 1930.
—*The Religion of China*, trans. by Gerth, 1951.
—*The Religion of India*, trans. by Gerth and Martindale, 1967.
—*Ancient Judaism*, trans. by Gerth and Martindale, 1952.

11. G. le Bras, *Introduction à l'histoire de la pratique réligieuse en France*, 1942. See also works by F. Boulard, H. Carrier and E. Pin.

2

THE DEFINITION OF RELIGION:
RELIGION AND COMMUNITY

It is readily accepted by students that all known societies have been to some degree religious. This acceptance should imply agreement as to just what constitutes religious behaviour, but in fact agreement on this point has been harder to obtain. Argument on how to define religion, and on how to mark it off on the one hand from magic, science and philosophy, and from some kinds of political and social enthusiasm on the other, has continued for many years. This, in spite of substantial agreement in practice on the range and type of data which the sociologist of religion should try to handle.

E. B. Tylor in his pioneer study *Primitive Culture*, published in 1871, put forward what he called a 'minimum definition' of religion that would not prejudge further questions as to its source or function. He defined it as 'a belief in spiritual beings'.[1] But dissatisfaction was expressed with this on the ground that it was too intellectualist, and did not refer to the specifically religious emotions of awe and reverence which were associated with such beliefs. Tylor's definition was further criticised because it seemed to imply that the objects of the religious attitude were always personal beings, whereas accumulating anthropological evidence suggested that the spiritual was often conceived of as an impersonal power. Radcliffe-Brown, an anthropologist of a much later period, offers a definition which tries to make good these supposed deficiencies. 'Religion', he says, 'is everywhere an expression in one form or another of a sense of dependence on a power outside ourselves, a power of which we may speak as a spiritual or moral power.'[2] For him, the crucial expression of this sense of dependence was ritual. He stressed the definiteness

of rituals, and of the social obligation to perform them, in contrast
to the indefiniteness and variability in the beliefs concerning the
objects of ritual. In this he stands very near to Durkheim, who
insisted on the collective or social character of religion in his definition. To him, 'religion is a unified system of beliefs and practices
relative to sacred things, that is to say, things set apart and forbidden
—beliefs and practices which unite into a single moral community
called a church all those who adhere to them'.[3] He does not, at the
point of definition, further analyse the word sacred, and his critics
have said that the notion of the sacred is too vague and shifting to be
a satisfactory element in the definition of religion. However, it does
become clear in his whole work that 'the sacred' which is 'set apart
and forbidden' is that which can only be approached by ritual,
because its power can be dangerous as well as beneficent. The
movement from the profane everyday world to the presence of the
sacred has to be undertaken cautiously, and only in socially approved
ways. Thus ritual and the emotions of fear and awe are to Durkheim,
as to Radcliffe-Brown, the basic qualities of religion, regardless of
the objects of ritual.

A further step away from defining religion by referring only to
beliefs was taken by those who explicitly chose a functional definition.
The contemporary American sociologist, Yinger, declares that he
prefers 'functional to valuative or substantive definitions', and goes
on to aver that 'religion is a system of beliefs and practices by means
of which a group of people struggles with the ultimate problems of
human life. It is the refusal to capitulate to death, to give up in face
of frustration, to allow hostility to tear apart one's human associations.'[4] (Tillich, the philosopher, travels along part of the same road
when he asserts that religion is that which is of ultimate concern.)
It is clear that both sentences of Yinger's definition must be read
together, otherwise it would cover not only religion but philosophy,
science and technology as well. Taking it as a whole, it is clearly a
maximum rather than a minimum definition, since it incorporates
the view that religion enables men to struggle successfully against
anxiety and hate. What constitutes success here is very difficult to
judge, but it is evident from the rest of Yinger's work that he is
among those who stress that man, among all the animal kingdom,
is the only worrier, that his intelligence produces more perplexities
than it can solve. Functionalist definitions such as Yinger's correspond to the view that rational thought cannot answer questions of the
meaning of life, even though these questions can only be posed by a
rational being. The leap of religious faith is therefore seen as an

alternative to despair. Since this view entails the conclusion that religion is a constant factor in human life, the definition which corresponds to it is cast in wide terms which allow almost any kind of enthusiastic purpose or strong loyalty, provided it is shared by a group, to count as religion. The object of belief, and the importance of ritual, are left out, as also the idea of a specifically religious emotion, though this last may be implied in the view that through their religious behaviour men move from anxiety to confidence.

Another writer who sees religion as depending on the peculiar characteristics of man as a creature without clearly defined instincts, and with a strong exploratory intelligence, is the contemporary anthropologist, Geertz. He defines religion as 'a system of symbols which acts to establish powerful, pervasive and long-lasting moods and motivations in men by formulating concepts of a general order of existence, and clothing these conceptions with such an aura of factuality that the moods and motivations seem uniquely realistic'.[5] When he discusses the ways in which the symbols and concepts are 'clothed with such an aura of factuality' he gives a quite Durkheimian prominence to collective ritual, though leaving other possibilities open. His definition has the advantage of bringing clearly into the ambit of religious phenomena those political or moral movements in which collective rituals play an important part, and in which the participants, while not accepting that they are making a leap of faith beyond the limits of reasoned conviction, do in fact feel that their 'concepts of a general order of existence' make their 'moods and motivations seem uniquely realistic'. Nationalist, Communist and Fascist movements fall quite easily within this definition. At the same time it delimits the field more closely than Yinger's formulation, and is more in accordance with prevailing usage, since only symbols and concepts 'of a general order of existence' are to be considered as religious.

It is interesting to see in Geertz's definition a reversion to the emphasis on beliefs. This is even more apparent in a recent attempt at a qualified Tylorian 'minimum definition' by Goody.[6] 'Religious beliefs,' he says, 'are present when non-human agencies are propitiated on the human model. Religious activities are not only the acts of propitiation themselves, but all behaviour which has reference to the existence of these agencies.' Here belief is clearly the central factor, and the writer attempts to get over the difficulties of applying the sacred/profane, or supernatural/natural dichotomies by using the negative category of 'non-human' to describe the objects of belief. The emotional and ritual elements are brought in by the use of the word propitiation to describe the central act of the believer. But is Goody correct when he argues that his definition is in fact what is 'employed in practice by the majority of writers in this field, whatever expressed theory they have adopted'? It clearly covers all the historically known religions, and also the religious practices of preliterate peoples, and these two kinds of data have been at the centre of the sociologist's concern. Yet many writers, from Durkheim onward, have wished to include Nationalism and other intense political loyalties in their category of religious behaviour, and Goody's definition hardly permits this, since acts of propitiation are not their central feature, and their human leaders may not claim, or be endowed by their followers with, non-human characteristics. Yet it seems likely that the hero-worship which in ancient history led to leaders being credited with non-human attributes, for example the power to work miracles, was not different in quality from the intense devotion which some modern political leaders have received. Also, as I hope to show in a later chapter, such functional theories of religion as have been developed all tend to take for their province a wider field of data than Goody's definition covers.

Whatever positive definition of religion they have adopted, sociologists, and particularly anthropologists, have tried to distinguish between magic and religion. The agreed distinction is basically between religion as the propitiation or worship of non-human or sacred objects, and magic as the manipulation or control of such objects. It is granted that in practice the two attitudes may mingle or alternate, or that certain participants in a rite may conceive it in the religious mode, while others, using the same words and actions, may understand it magically. Thus the act of sacrifice may be looked upon as a way of showing submission and adoration, or as a bargain by which the giver of the sacrifice binds the god to grant his wish in return. It is also possible to find basically religious philosophies in which magical elements play a recognised part, and cannot be looked on merely as corruptions of true doctrine by the untutored masses. Such is the case with the old Hindu doctrine that only by priestly performance of ritual will the power of the gods be maintained. But the combination or confusion of magical and religious elements in one system of thought does not make the conceptual distinction between the two useless or unworkable.

The distinction of religion from science, philosophy and ethics naturally follows from all definitions of religion which lay stress on emotional attitude or ritual. It is possible to elaborate a philosophy, morality or science in which emotions of awe and rites of propitiation play no part. In practice, however, in nearly all systems of thought, religious belief and its philosophical and ethical defence or elaboration have been closely linked. In the modern world these links are weaker, or absent, and therefore it seems necessary to distinguish conceptually religion, ethics, philosophy and science. But conceptual distinctness should not imply disconnectedness in practice.

If it is difficult to agree on a definition of religion, it must be correspondingly difficult to agree on the meaning and application of the terms secular or secularisation. I propose to distinguish three ways in which these words are used, and to try to show how these uses are related to the limited definition of religion put forward by Goody, and to the more inclusive conception of Geertz.

Secularisation may first of all be used with an institutional reference, to describe a process of separation of religious from political, legal, economic or other institutions. This meaning is nearest to the original use of the term to describe the removal from ecclesiastical control of lands and lordships in sixteenth-century Germany after the Reformation. A full degree of secularisation in this sense would mean that roles in non-religious institutions required no religious qualification and had no religious components. Conversely, the incumbents of religious roles would not, because of this incumbency, hold any positions in non-religious institutions. The processes of separation of church from state which have taken place in many European countries, and which are constitutionally guaranteed the USA, are examples of secularisation in this first sense. It is also applicable in this sense even in situations where there has never been any church organisation of the type known to Christendom. Thus the Turkish abolition of the Moslem caliphate in 1924, and the simultaneous rejection of the political power traditionally wielded by the ulema, the body of Moslem theologians and lawyers, were striking examples of secularisation. So also was the proclamation of the new independent India in 1948 as a secular state. The Brahmin castes had never constituted a priesthood in the Christian sense, nor formed an ecclesiastical organisation remotely comparable to the churches of Christendom. Nevertheless, compared with the position during and before British rule in India, the post-1948 position is very much more secular, since membership of Hindu, Moslem or other religious group has no bearing on civil or political status, and the privileges of the Brahmins are not backed by the power of the state.

It is common to conceive of secularisation in this sense as a one-way and irreversible process, as part of a general development of institutional differentiation, but this is an unsafe generalisation, even on the basis of a narrow definition of religion. There have certainly been periods in Chinese and Japanese history in which Buddhist monasteries have grown in political and economic power, and become institutionally more closely linked with the ruling class. In the institutional sense Tibet was less secular in the period 1642 to 1959 than in the years before and after. It is certainly arguable that the Christian Roman Empire of Constantine and his successors was much less secular than the pagan empire of the preceding three centuries. Even in very recent history there are some counter-examples to the trend towards secularisation. Spain, after the civil war of 1936–8, moved from separation back to linkage of church and state. Pakistan was founded as an Islamic state, and continues to regard itself as such. Burma, upon regaining its independence, took steps to re-establish and show favour, financially and otherwise, to Buddhism.

If our wider definition of religion is used, then the so-called trend to secularisation shows even more exceptions, for Fascism and Communism in power fall within the definition of religions, and these regimes have deliberately made the party, or the movement, the means by which all institutions, right down to the family, are linked, coordinated and supervised.

According to this first sense of secular, it would be reasonable to talk of a secular, as contrasted with a religious, state or economy, and equally reasonable to distinguish between religious music, art or scholarship, and their secular counterparts. But it would not be reasonable to talk of a secular society, for it is quite possible to conceive a society in which religious institutions are distinct and separate, but in which there is very widespread participation in religious practices, and the majority of people are members of religious groups. The USA today approximates to this position. It would be clearly misleading in such a case to use the phrase 'secular society' and when this term is used, there is an extension of meaning in two directions. The first is to indicate a withdrawal from religious participation and affiliation. A society is more secular in this sense if fewer people regularly attend religious services, make use of religious *rites de passage*, or join and support religious organisations. This kind of secularisation, or religiosity, can be assessed by church membership figures, attendance at services, choice of religious or civil marriage or burial. The degree of secularisation (or its reverse) in this sense is fairly easy to observe in respect of well-established organisations; it is more difficult in respect of new ones, whose religious character may be disputed because they show different types of belief and ritual. Or there may be increased popularity of certain beliefs agreed to be religious, but no corresponding organisation or ritual. How far should Western sympathisers with Zen Buddhism be counted as 'believers', and given the same weight in the statistics as the Catholic who goes to mass, or the Anglican making his Easter communion? Scientology shows a high degree of structured, even ritual, behaviour, but not all its practitioners, nor those outside it, would agree that it is a religion. It is clear that in contemporary societies we would get two different measures of secularisation in this second sense, according to whether we chose to apply the minimum or the more inclusive definition of religion. In the first case we would discover a very great degree of secularisation; in the second, either a lesser degree, or, in the case of some totalitarian countries, a movement in the opposite direction. Nevertheless, once a definition of religion is chosen and consistently applied, I believe the term secular, in this second sense of assessing participation or abstention from religion, to be useful and not misleading. Using either definition of religion, it would be reasonable to say that today the USA is a more religious society than Britain, or that Sweden is more secular than Holland.

The second extension of meaning which may be involved in the phrase 'secular society' is in respect of beliefs, categories of thought, attitudes to science and morality, general world-views. It has been argued that contemporary Western society, particularly the USA, is secular in this sense, regardless of its varying habits of church-going or church-joining. Clearly this is a most important use of the term, but one upon which it is very difficult to agree, since it is not only a matter of searching out the evidence, but deciding what sort of evidence is relevant. Since those who argue for a high degree of secularisation in this third sense usually contend that the religious world-view is replaced by a materialist or scientific world-view, the question can also be approached by asking whether a scientific world-view is widely held. But this raises further questions as to the assumptions, methods, and limitations of science, and how far these are understood beyond the body of scientists, or even by them. Take for example the evidence of persistent belief in folk-superstitions, such as the luckiness of a black cat, or in purely personal ones, such as belief in a lucky number. At what level of conviction are these beliefs held? Do the believers attempt to reconcile them with a belief in the authority of the natural sciences, or with their religious beliefs? Martin suggests that superstitious beliefs are prevalent in Britain today, and that this is evidence against secularisation of thought.[7] Others disagree and argue that as these beliefs are not incorporated in any important social customs or institutions, they cannot be central to the world-view of those believers.

Another question about relevant evidence concerns attitudes to moral rules and values. It is true that in recent centuries a utilitarian or hedonist ethic has often been associated with scepticism or hostility to Christianity. But it would be a bold man who would generalise from this and infer that anyone who professes that moral judgements should be made according to the consequences of actions should be deemed irreligious and secular, while those who hold to an ethic of absolute rights and duties should be considered religious. Should the Declaration of the Rights of Man be taken as a religious or counter-religious document?

A third matter requiring investigation would be the kinds of interpretation which religious believers give to their creeds and rituals. What do they take literally, and what symbolically? And what range of symbolic interpretations is to be counted within the category of religious belief? The Confucian system contains firm ethical rules and ritual prescriptions, but recommends abstention from metaphysical speculation about the nature or reality of a world of spirits. Is it to be classed as a more secular system of thought than one replete with theological dogmas? Does the 'demythologisation' of Christianity which has been taken so far by some writers necessarily involve 'the death of Christianity by a thousand qualifications', or is it a clearer restatement of the essence of Christian belief? These questions and many others are involved in the concepts of religious and secular world-views.

Those sociologists, such as Martin,[8] who are very critical of the muddled use of the term secularisation, base their criticisms largely on the fact that the evidence for the kind of world-view people have is never properly marshalled and examined, and that evidence for the first kind of secularisation (institutional separation) and for the second (decline in religious affiliation and practice) is too easily taken as evidence for the third kind also.

Nevertheless these critics would agree on one aspect of the substitution of a secular for a religious world-view. They would accept that in industrial societies the advance of technology has enormously reduced the tendency to explain every event by reference to gods and demons, spells and prayers. The god, or gods, who remain as objects of belief are still propitiated, but not on such a variety of occasions. They may be regarded as continually intervening in the moral and social order, but not in the natural order. The idea of chance is accepted, together with the concept of natural laws, and the idea of providential or magical intervention vanishes. This change of attitude concerning the relation of God and his creation may be due to the greater security from natural disasters which industrial societies enjoy; whatever the reason, it is probably a powerful influence towards making religious beliefs more effectively monotheistic, and thus lowering any barriers to scientific advance which remaining magical or animistic beliefs might present. The process therefore feeds upon itself. So far the argument is that advancing science and technology involve a change in religion, but not necessarily a decline. Those who think that it does also entail a decline point to the empirical association found between the two phenomena, and interpret it in terms of cause and effect. But many social changes take place during the forward march of technology in an industrialising society, and there are several possible intervening variables between the supposedly associated factors of technical advance and religious decline. I would accept, however, that using the minimum definition of religion taken from Goody, advancing technology does, directly and indirectly, limit the sphere of influence of the gods, and sets alongside religious belief a new and greater confidence in human potentialities. This greater confidence can be termed, again in relation to Goody's definition, a secular component of the world-view of members of such societies.

The irony is that as this confidence in human powers, human science and human brotherhood grows, so it tends to become religious, at least in the more inclusive usage of the term. Or, rather, there grows out of this Promethean confidence and hope a specific faith in a supposedly scientific theory of society, say Marxism, or in a leader who promises Utopia, say Hitler or Hubbard, or in a humanist ethic which believes that a direct appeal to the brotherhood of man may succeed, where an appeal through the fatherhood of God has failed.

The reasons why in the field of human affairs a scientific detachment, a willingness to admit ignorance and revise errors, are so difficult to maintain, are themselves matters of dispute and uncertainty. But the fact of our impatience and enthusiasm cannot be doubted, and therefore the impossibility of the world-view of any society being thoroughly secular has to be accepted. Such a world-view may or may not give rise to the 'propitiation of non-human agencies'; it certainly contains within it 'a system of symbols which acts to establish powerful, pervasive, and long-lasting moods and motivations in men'.

I turn now to two major tasks in the sociology of religion. The first is to examine the relation of social wholes, civilisations or total societies to religious systems. Do religious systems transcend particular communities or coincide with them? The second is to examine the degree and kind of specialisation of religious roles in different societies and religious systems. I suggest that there are three ways in which a religion may be linked with a social whole. The first is that participation in the group's rituals and knowledge of its beliefs is an inseparable aspect of group membership. To be a member of the community involves worshipping the gods of the community. The second is that the system of belief and ritual is specific to a community; the same pattern is not to be found outside it. The third is that the rituals and beliefs should refer particularly to the history and fate of that particular community, and not to mankind at large, or to the individual considered as such. But to apply any of these criteria we need also to establish what the effective social whole is, by some test other than participation in a particular religious pattern, and this is not easy to do except in the case of some quite isolated preliterate peoples. The tests which are commonly applied are those of common language, identification of membership by the people concerned, and common allegiance to a ruler or a set of rules preserving peace within the group. These tests do not all yield the same result in every case; in what follows I try to discuss social wholes in the light of the third criterion, which might be called a political one.

Where the social whole, so defined, has its own religion in all the three senses I have outlined, the religion may be termed fully communal. But we have already noticed one respect in which no religion is fully communal; all peoples have some notion of a 'high God' who creates or maintains the order of the world, and whose concerns and power go beyond the fate or origin of one particular group. We have also noted that such a deity, particularly among preliterate peoples, may be unimportant or completely omitted as an object of ritual. Where this is the case we are likely to find examples of the most communal type of religion.

By the first criterion it might be argued that the religions of all preliterate peoples are communal. To grow up in the society, to marry, to show obedience to a chief, to inherit or bequeath goods, to carry out the obligations of kinship, may all involve accepting the gods and spirits, the rites and sacrifices, of that particular community.

The history of recent Christian missions to preliterate societies shows how closely religious behaviour was interwoven with social structure in all its aspects. The converts had to leave their old community and found a new one, if they were to take their new religious obligations seriously. Nevertheless it might be argued that the history of a great part of Buddhist, Islamic, Hindu and even Christian expansion shows the reverse, i.e., that primitive religions were not so communal that new beliefs necessarily disrupted the community or forced the believer into an eccentric or ostracised position. The apparent contradiction can be resolved by showing how the new religion was in the one case presented as a substitute, in the other as an addition to previous beliefs and practices. Since the old communal religion will already contain some belief in a high God, it is possible for the single God of Islam or Christianity to be identified with this high God; provided he makes no ethical or ritual demands in conflict with existing practice, the new belief is hardly more than a renaming of the old. Similar identifications can also be seen in the process of Hinduisation of primitive religions in tribal India. In the case of Buddhism, the new could also be represented as an addition rather than a substitute for the old, since Buddhism proclaimed a special knowledge of the way to salvation rather than a special dogma of the reality of one God and the falsity of others. We may conclude that the coincidence of religious and social membership in preliterate societies has not prevented individuals, or even whole groups, in such societies from adding to their religious repertoire. But the addition of some compatible aspects of a world religion such as Buddhism, Christianity or Islam does nevertheless represent an alteration of the original structure of the community. Barriers have been lowered, and membership in a wider society has been accepted. This acceptance may seem perfectly compatible with the fulfilment of one's duties to clan, village or tribe, but it may nevertheless gradually alter their content. Thus it has been observed that in sub-Saharan Africa a very gradual process of Islamisation has gone on, with little direct challenge of pagan communal religions by mono-theism. Allah is added, not substituted. But if the obligation of pilgrimage to Mecca is undertaken, the returning pilgrim is a man who has seen much more of the world than his fellows. He may become the focus of innovation, of challenge to the traditional leadership, and thus may change the old social structure. The fact that adherence to a world religion gives access to literacy is also of enormous importance in weakening isolation, and thus altering the structure of the community.

Communal religion in the first sense, of religion as an aspect of community membership, is not confined to preliterate societies. In fact it is so widespread as to give force to Durkheim's belief that religious symbols are representations of society and nothing else. The city-states of the Greek world and of Babylonian civilisation each had their protecting deity, and to be a citizen was to participate in his worship. Confucianism, taken as that group of cults of which Confucian philosophers approved, was a communal religion in which participation in cults of family, city and empire was part of the duty of the subject, and the mark of acceptance of paternal and imperial authority. Even the other world religions have sometimes taken on this aspect of communalism. To the Russian, baptism in the Orthodox church was a rite of membership in the Russian nation. To the majority of Poles the Catholic faith is an inseparable part of their nationhood; a Magyar proverb existed to the effect that to be Magyar was to be Calvinist. The alliance between the Presbyterian form of Protestantism and the Scottish sense of nationhood was once very strong, and even now still lives, as does the link between Catholic Christianity and Irish nationhood. Anglicans, at least up to the nineteenth century, looked upon membership in their church as the religious aspect of membership in the English nation. But in all these Christian cases, the identity of religion and society is now a matter of sentiment among the members of the society, rather than direct implication of religious practice in all kinds of social relations. The non-Catholic Pole and the non-Presbyterian Scot exist and have the same legal status and capacities as other members of their societies; social relations may be hampered but are not made impossible by the religious difference. This is very different from the communal religions of preliterate societies and ancient civilisations.

The clearest case of a communal religion in the first sense persisting into the modern world is that of orthodox Judaism. Long after the fall of the Jewish state, communities of Jews with administrative autonomy, and clear insulation from gentile society, persisted, and I think it realistic to claim that Jewry was an effective social whole to its members during all the centuries between the conquest of Palestine by Rome and the modern movements of emancipation and assimilation. Religious and social membership coincided, and to renounce the religion was to be expelled from the community. Judaism is an example of the persistence of communal religion in the first sense; Mormonism and Sikhism are equally striking examples of the creation of new communal religions, or religious communities. In the case of the Mormons, the religious difference led to physical separation of the new body of believers, and this, as much as the peculiarities of doctrine, led to the construction of a distinct community. In the Sikh case, the leaders attempted a monotheistic reformation of Hinduism, under the influence of Islam in India. But under pressure from Moslem rulers and orthodox Hindus, the followers of the new doctrines became more and more clearly distinguishable as a separate community, with its own rituals and its own political rulers.

Let us now turn to the application of the second criterion of a communal religion, i.e., that the system of belief and ritual is specific to a community. This must of course be true of such religions as Mormonism, Sikhism and Judaism, where the community is based on religious differentiation. But it also holds in the case of many other religions which are also communal in our first sense. Most preliterate societies have a system of beliefs and cults not practised outside their boundaries. However, it should be emphasised that the borrowing of mythical and ritual items is not unknown even in societies where religious and social membership coincide. It appears that the fit between religious system and social structure is not so close that a single cult cannot be detached from its original setting and implanted successfully in a neighbouring one. So long as the basic framework of thought is animistic or polytheistic there is no great obstacle to the import of new cults; an additional worship addressed to a more powerful god may seem pragmatically justified. There may be loss as well as gain, although the time span of anthropological research can only show this happening in relation to the invasion of paganism by such world religions as Christianity and Islam. In West Africa, Parrinder's conclusion is that while rites addressed to nature spirits die out quickly under the influence of Christianity or Islam, the cults which reflect social loyalties to kin and chiefs are more persistent.[9] The frequency of borrowing and syncretism, of loss and gain of particular items, again suggests that even in the simple preliterate societies there is a relatively loose connection of religion with social structure. At any point of time the religious system may be specific to the particular community, yet its components may vary over time in response to external contacts.

The detachability of cults from particular societies can be seen clearly in Graeco–Roman civilisation. It was one of the traditional oracles of Roman society which advised the importation of the Phrygian goddess Cybele to Rome as an aid to the defeat of Carthage. The worship of Persian Mithra spread throughout the Roman

Empire, as earlier the cult of Dionysus had spread from Thrace southward through the Greek world. Though population movement no doubt contributed to the separation of cult from community, this separation was not a simple effect of migration. Rather it seems that in a more geographically mobile and large-scale society, there were more people no longer satisfied with the communal religion of their particular city or tribe, who were ready to experiment with new kinds of religion. To participate in any of these foreign mystery religions was neither a mark of citizenship nor a derogation from it, because they were not communal religions in either the first or second senses I have distinguished.

In the second sense the world religions of Christianity and Buddhism are the least communal. To give them the name of world religion is to imply that they count their adherents in many different communities. Some points of doctrine, some similarities of ritual, can be seen throughout their history and across the whole span of members; otherwise it would be misleading to refer to them as single religions. Nevertheless, in each of them there are many variations on the common themes, and often the group practising a particular variation is a distinct community. We may again take Mormonism as a variant of Christianity where the religious message forms the basis of the community, but the cases are more numerous where Christianity has been interpreted to defend the interests or express the loyalties of pre-existing communities. The theological disputes of the early Christian church reflected the rivalries of Rome, Egypt, Syria and Constantinople within the Empire. The theological causes of schism between Eastern and Western Christendom were also expressions of rivalry and hostility between Greek and Latin-speaking countries. The case of the heretical Donatist church in North Africa during the fourth to sixth centuries A.D. is an interesting one; it has been interpreted both as a protest of Berber peasantry against Romanised city-dwellers, and as a movement to a distinct community based on a religious dispute about the proper qualities of the priesthood and the true nature of God's church on earth. In Buddhism there has been more coexistence with other faiths, and therefore less chance of political and social loyalties taking the form of a special variety of Buddhism. Certainly, the main line of division in faith and practice, that between Mahayana and Hinayana Buddhism, does not run along any political or linguistic divide. However, Tibetan Buddhism does seem to be one clear case where a specific kind of religious practice is linked with a particular community.

Islam is a religion which originally transformed rather than created a community. It has always retained the theocratic ideal that the boundaries of religious faith and political community should coincide. Yet for two reasons the ideal has not been attained. Rapid expansion of Islam by soldiers, traders and missionaries has incorporated many diverse communities, including some who resisted conversion and some only superficially Islamised. On the other hand, strains and tensions within the enlarged community of the faithful led to political divisions, each of which became the basis of a more or less distinct community. The common faith did not prevent the development of separate or distinct communities in, for instance, Egypt, India, and the Turkish Empire.

In Hinduism, Taoism and Confucianism we have three religions in which a strongly communal aspect, in the sense of a tie with a particular community, is observable. We think of Hinduism as inseparable from Indian society; Confucianism and Taoism as inseparable from Chinese. Yet we need to recognise that each of these religions, in encompassing so many peoples over such enormous territories, has in fact shown something of the footloose missionary quality of Buddhism, Christianity and Islam. The old Vedic religion of the Aryan immigrants has become the Hindu religion of Aryan and non-Aryan in the sub-continent, and has influenced religious systems in Burma, Cambodia and Indonesia as well. The capacity of Confucianism and Taoism to influence the great variety of peoples who have either invaded China from the north, or been subjected to the southward pressure of the Chinese Empire, proves that neither of these systems is narrowly communal. Confucianism as a system of ritual sanctified the political system of empire; in that sense it was very closely linked to a particular community. Taoism was much less committed to any particular form of social organisation; its beliefs and rites, like those of the mystery religions in the Graeco–Roman world, drew individuals together to form congregations within the wider community. Yet members of these could also follow the more communally based Confucian rites. Transiently, Taoism seems to have inspired rebellions against the Confucian imperial order, just as Christian sects and heresies have expressed dissatisfaction and revolt against church and state. But such rebellions have not led to the setting up of distinct and long-lasting Taoist communities.

To sum up: large-scale communities do not show religious homogeneity. There are many relics of small-scale communal loyalties within them, and many varieties of religious congregations which stop short of developing into distinct communities. This is so even in the case of Indian and Chinese civilisation where the traditional nomenclature of Hinduism and Confucianism emphasises the limitation of a religion to a particular society. In fact each comprises a variety of cults, in Hinduism by incorporation and reinterpretation of non-Aryan systems, in Confucianism by toleration of many varieties of Taoism and Buddhism. Also it should be noted that Hinduism has always transcended the limits of political communities, just as Christianity and Buddhism have done.

The third suggested criterion for a communal religion is that its rituals and beliefs should refer prominently, if not exclusively, to a particular community, rather than to mankind as a whole or to individuals. Again, by this test, the religions of the preliterate peoples stand out as more communal than those of literate and larger-scale societies. Yet, even in this third sense, communal aspects of religion can be traced in all civilisations. Within their religious heterogeneity, which we have just noted, it is usually possible to identify some beliefs and cults particularly concerned with the prosperity and survival of the community. In the case of Confucianism these cults and the associated ethical teaching in fact constitute the whole religion. The same could be said of Japanese Shintoism. In the cases of Christianity and Buddhism, whose original message is both individual and universal, the adaptation of these religions to the uses of patriotism or emperor-worship is usually looked upon as distortion and corruption. It is expected that such bondage is temporary and reversible, but the history of both religions shows that it is a recurrent phenomenon. The modification of the universalist and individualist gospel to fit the purpose of exalting a particular community or ruler has been effected without alteration of basic creeds or rituals, but a significant addition is made. The particular community or ruler is deemed to be the divinely chosen defender or exemplar of the faith, without whose exertions mankind will not be brought to accept the true religion. Christianity, relying on an allegorical treatment of Old Testament history and New Testament prophecy, shows many examples of this idea. The conception of a 'new Israel', a new chosen people of God, enables group loyalty and religious universalism to be reconciled. Buddhism lays less stress on history in its sacred texts, yet has discovered other ways of effecting this reconciliation. Thus the Buddhism of Ceylon and Tibet has been permeated with the idea of the nation as the defender of the faith, and the source of religious influence on surrounding peoples. Nichiren taught a version of Buddhism in Japan which emphasised the special capacity of the Japanese to fulfil the Buddhist teaching.

Islam and Judaism, in law and ritual, emphasise the religious value of the community without denying God's concern for all mankind. Islam proclaims the ideal of bringing everyone to the true faith; the community of the faithful is the supreme earthly value, but ideally this comprises all mankind. Judaism, averse to proselytising, has developed the idea of a covenant of the chosen people with God, by which they are bound to a law and ritual applying only to the community. By perfect fulfilment of it they can become a holy people, fit to be used by God for the redemption of all mankind.

Hinduism stands at the opposite pole from Buddhism and Christianity in respect of the third criterion of communal religion. Far from group rituals and loyalties being, as in the latter case, a corruption of universalist religion, they are the raw materials of a subsequent transformation towards a more universalist type. While rituals still concern themselves overtly with such groups as family, caste or kingdom, the over-arching beliefs which give some unity to the system are concerned purely with the individual and his understanding of ultimate reality, and his way to release from the cycle of earthly existences.

I now turn to the question of specialisation of religious roles in different systems. Specialisation in religious roles seems to have been one of the earliest and most widespread forms of the division of labour in human society. But even where priests and diviners exist, it is quite possible that some religious duties will fall to heads of families, chiefs, nobles and kings, sometimes even to young children or old women.

In preliterate societies the priest appears as a specialist in ritual in all its aspects, including the interpretation of oracles and the practice of healing. A distinction between the individual magician and his clients, and the body of priests carrying out rites on behalf of the whole society is generally visible, although some of the collective rites may bear a magical rather than a religious interpretation. The leaders of the community, or of groups within it such as lineages or villages, also have some ritual responsibilities, which they may discharge unaided, or with the help of priests. Furthermore, in these societies, the priest may very well be a farmer or herder most of his time. The degree of specialisation is therefore slight, and the priest not set apart very clearly from the rest of the community.

In the ancient civilisations the differentiation of priests, and their corporate organisation, were probably more marked. Priestly roles were often very wide, and included not only ritual and the study and copying of sacred texts, but calculation of the calendar, public record-keeping and the safe-keeping of valuables, public and private, deposited in the temples. The priests were the learned class, providing some or all the administrative staff of the ruler. In this kind of social structure, it is clear that the priesthood could emerge as a particular interest group in the society, rather than as the servants of ruler and community. The position of the priests of Delphi *vis-à-vis* the rivalrous Greek city-states, the enormous power of the priesthood in ancient Persia, and the vested interests of the priests in maintaining local cults in Pharaonic Egypt, are just three historical cases in which this possibility was actualised.

Further understanding of the part played by religious specialists in the great world religions can perhaps be achieved by using two principles of classification. The first, whether religious roles are ascribed by sex or birth, or whether they are achieved by personal qualification. The second, what kind and degree of special qualities are attributed to religious functionaries.

In those two religions least closely linked with particular communities, Christianity and Buddhism, religious roles have in theory always been achieved, not ascribed. The Christian priest, monk or nun takes personal vows and is ceremonially inducted into his or her new status, which, in the case of the Catholic priest, carries with it the capacity to perform certain sacramental rites indispensable to all believers. For this induction there is no qualification or disqualification by birth. The Christian leader of an order, denomination or sect also achieves his position of religious leadership by personal success in gathering adherents around him. In Buddhism the central institution is the monastic order, which all men and women are in theory free to enter, regardless of birth.

Even in religions where the tie to a community is much stronger, there are many achieved roles. The Moslem specialists in sacred law, the ulema, and the leaders of public prayers, the imams, are trained for their roles and do not inherit them. The role of caliph, the supreme head of the politico-religious community of Islam, which existed from the death of Mohammed until 1924, is more difficult to characterise as achieved or ascribed, since Moslems themselves have differed about the proper choice of a caliph. In actual history the office tended to pass much like a secular kingship, by succession in a dynasty, but with jumps from one dynasty to another through power struggles between them. The role of shaykh, or holy man, within Islam has borne a partly ascriptive, partly achieved character. A new leader might arise, gathering round him followers who believed in his claims to sanctity, to visions and ecstasies and miracle-working powers. But his success would begin a dynasty of shaykhs, since holiness of this kind was deemed to be inheritable.

In Judaism the rabbi appears as a specialist in sacred law and leader of public worship; his position is achieved, not ascribed by birth. The prophets of ancient Judaism, who transformed the religion from tribal monolatry to ethical monotheism, appear to have been leaders who achieved the traditional roles of seer and diviner, but played them in a new way, combining the old function of foretelling the future with the new one of social critic and religious innovator. Certainly birth played no part in their qualifications.

Hinduism also shows some achieved religious roles, in spite of Brahmanic theory. The guru, the leader who, like the Moslem shaykh, makes a personal appeal and gathers a personal following, does not need to come from a Brahmin caste. He has been a persistent figure in Hindu history.

Finally we may note that in Confucianism the system of appointing administrators by examination was also a system of achieved priestly roles, since the administrators were the servants of the Emperor in carrying out the Confucian rituals.

Looking now at the distribution of ascribed roles, we may note that the tie of religion to community, particularly to political community, seems to go with some degree of ascription of roles. We have noted that the caliphate was nearest to an ascribed role in Islam, and this office, always in theory and often in practice, was the leadership of a theocratic state. While Jewish political independence lasted, the predominant religious role was played by the priests, and these could only be drawn from certain families in the community. In Confucianism, though administrators achieved their positions, the supreme priest was the Emperor himself, whose position was ascribed. (As in the case of the caliphate, theory and practice tended to diverge; from time to time the 'mandate of Heaven' fell on a usurper instead of a legitimate heir.) In Hinduism the role of priest is ascribed through membership in a Brahmin caste; though not all Brahmins actually perform religious functions for others, all are qualified by birth to do so.

It might be thought that in a system of celibate monasticism such as Buddhism it would be impossible in theory to ascribe religious roles by birth. It is therefore interesting to notice that in Tibet, the case where Buddhist monks wielded the greatest political power, and where the head of the state was a monk, the theory of reincarnation of souls was so used as to ascribe the roles of Dalai Lama and Panchen Lama to babies at birth.

Both in Christianity and Buddhism, whenever the religion has been closely tied to the fortunes of a particular state, the role of king has itself been given a sacred character, through coronation ceremonies and the like, and this role has, in theory at least, been ascribed, not achieved. I venture to suggest that where the political role of religion is prominent, there the allocation of religious roles by birth will occur.

The difference of theory and practice with regard to roles ideally looked upon as ascriptive has been noted in various contexts. The difference of theory and practice with regard to achieved roles should also be recognised. In general, if an element of ascription exists despite the theory, this is due to the influence of social stratification in non-religious roles. If religious roles give power, powerful men will want to adopt them, just as the wealthy aim at political power, and the politically powerful try to buttress their position by wealth. Even in celibate systems the desire to improve or maintain the social status of a family can lead to a strong element of ascription of religious roles. Leaders in the church and religious orders tend to be drawn from the upper social strata in the community. However, the corporate organisation of the priests or monks, the colleges of the ulema, may to some extent resist these pressures from the non-religious élites, as the Papacy has from time to time done in Christian history. Moreover the influence of secular wealth and power is less likely to be felt in those religious roles which have an element of innovation, even of rebellion, in them, such roles as the Christian sectarian, the Moslem shaikh, or the itinerant Buddhist monk preaching a new version of his faith. We may conclude that though the great religions have frequently sanctified a secular social structure of ascribed roles, their own functionaries have never been fully organised on this pattern.

As a footnote it is worth remarking that one ascriptive element, that of sex, is almost universal. Only in a few cases of Christian sectarianism and Moslem sufi orders does a woman appear as a religious leader on the same footing as a man. This has some relevance to theories of religion, particularly the Freudian.

We may now consider, not how religious positions are filled, but the degree to which they are differentiated from the laity. At one extreme we may put the orthodox Hindu position, in which only those born into a Brahmin caste may perform religious rites essential to the community. Priests are indispensable, and priestly quality is inborn and hereditary. The Catholic and Orthodox forms of Christianity agree that priests are essential, and link this belief with a theory of sacraments and of the unbroken succession of priests by ordination since the time of Christ. But the office of priest is separable from the personal qualities of the priest, and in extreme cases can be removed from a man. These forms of Christianity also show the separated groups of monks and nuns, again marked off by ceremony and personal vows from the laity. Buddhist priesthood is entirely monastic, and Buddhist monasticism differs from Christian in that there is greater ease in entering or leaving monastic life. Nevertheless the elders and abbots can be compared with Christian monks and priests in their distinct separation from the laity. The duty of monk to lay believer lies primarily in the field of ritual, though there is no sacramental theory to make this relation absolutely essential.

In Protestant Christianity the distinction between minister or priest and lay believer shows enormous variation. There is a recurrent tendency to assert the priesthood of all believers, and to limit the religious leader to a purely teaching or administrative role. Small sects may avoid any differentiation of roles at all. But the biggest Protestant groups, Lutheran, Calvinist and Anglican, have retained a priesthood shorn of some of the Catholic sacramental theory and practice. They have thus reduced, but not abolished, the difference between priest and layman.

Judaism is a case of a religion which has moved from a priesthood set apart by hereditary qualification and ritual indispensability, to religious leadership based primarily on learning. The rabbi's duties in leading public worship or in applying the sacred law do not mean that he requires special qualities conferred by birth or ordination. For a time in the post-Exilic Jewish commonwealth the rabbinic type of specialist coexisted with the temple priesthood; after the destruction of the temple in A.D. 70 only the rabbinate survived.

Islam has developed religious specialists who divide the functions of the Jewish rabbi. The ulema are the scholars of the sacred law and traditions, and the imams lead public worship. Neither are set apart as endowed with special personal qualities, or absolutely essential to the ritual life of the community. Heretical Shi'ite Islam has tended to attribute special qualities of holiness to the leaders of their community, but to orthodox Islam only the Caliph, as the representative on earth of Mohammed, was set apart from the body of believers.

It is apparent from this brief survey that each religion varies in the way priests or other religious specialists are distinguished from the main mass of believers. But there is one further type of relation of leader to led which seems to be discernible in each tradition, and that is the kind typified by the Hindu guru, the Moslem shaykh, the Chasidic rabbi of Eastern European Jewry, the Christian founder of an order or sect, and the Buddhist monk teaching a new method of achieving nirvana. The common element in all these cases seems to be that a relatively small group comes into being around a leader, who is believed to have special religious powers beyond those imputed to the priests, monks, rabbis or imams of the religious establishment. These special powers may be intellectual or moral, mystical or magical. This kind of leader and this kind of group occurs in all the great religions with the exception of Confucianism, and in this case it is obvious that Buddhism and Taoism, coexisting with Confucianism in China, can supply the deficiency. These groups may be partly institutionalised, as the shaikh or guru or itinerant Buddhist monk setting up on his own, but they also seem to be one of the instruments of change, and even revolution, in religion. Of the traditions we have been examining, it seems clear that three, Buddhism, Christianity and Islam, originated in just such an innovating and personal kind of religious leadership, the type which Weber called prophetic. It is not accidental that these three religions have the best claim to be called world religions, and are the least communal by any of the tests applied here. There are other smaller examples of this kind of development, for instance the Sikh faith breaking away from Hinduism, and the Ba'hais growing away from Islam. Much of the proliferating variety in Christianity, Buddhism, Islam and Hinduism can be traced to the same sort of beginnings.

1. E. B. Tylor, *Primitive Culture*, 1871.

2. A. Radcliffe-Brown, 'Religion and Society', *Journal of the Royal Anthropological Institute*, vol. LXXV, 1945.

3. E. Durkheim, *Elementary Forms of Religious Life*, 1964 ed., p. 47.

4. J. M. Yinger, *Religion, Society and the Individual*, 1957, p. 9.

5. C. Geertz, 'Religion as a Cultural System', from *Anthropological Approaches to the Study of Religion*, Ed. by M. Banton, p. 4.

6. J. Goody, 'Religion and Ritual; the Definitional Problem', *British Journal of Sociology*, vol. XII, 1961, pp. 157-8.

7. D. A. Martin, 'The Unknown Gods of the English', in *The Religious and the Secular*, 1969.

8. D. A. Martin, *The Religious and the Secular*, 1969.

9. G. Parrinder, *African Traditional Religion*, 1954.

3

THE STUDY OF RELIGION IN

SMALL-SCALE SOCIETIES

The study of religion in the small-scale societies analysed by social anthropologists can conveniently be seen in terms of its development from Durkheim's pioneer work. As we have seen, Durkheim concluded that religious objects were symbols of society, their sacredness deriving from the power that society as a whole exerted over each member, and their function being to preserve and invigorate the sense of social solidarity and social obligation. He tried to explain the 'sacredness' of magical objects as derivative from the sacredness of religious ones. Once it had come to be believed that a sacred power was inherent in, or attached to, a certain thing or form of words, men would try to use this power for individual or even anti-social ends, as well as for collective ends. This distortion of the true end of a rite was for Durkheim the essence of magic, as distinct from religion. For him, the typical magic rite was of the form of the 'black mass', where sacred things and words are perverted to anti-social ends.

His pupils and immediate successors tested out his ideas in different societies, and developed more fully his theory of magic. For instance, Hubert and Mauss studied Eskimo societies having a marked seasonal rhythm of dispersion and concentration, and tried to show that religious rituals only took place during the time when people lived closely together, and were an effect of this greater sociability.[1] They also undertook a fuller treatment of magic, showing how individual practitioners depended for their success on the collective nature of magical beliefs; magician, client and public all shared in the same system of thought. Durkheim's followers did not confine themselves to anthropological data only. Hubert and Mauss studied aspects of Judaism and of the Vedic religion of ancient

India,[2] and Jane Harrison and other English classical scholars enthusiastically interpreted classical Greek religion on Durkheimian lines.[3]

However, in the long term, Durkheim's main influence has been on the sociology of religion in primitive societies, which since his day has been developed almost entirely by those who have had actual experience of living and working among primitive peoples, learning their languages and trying to see things through their eyes. Radcliffe-Brown was one of those. He found that the ideas he had developed during his fieldwork among the Andaman islanders chimed in to a large extent with Durkheim's theories. Radcliffe-Brown dismissed that part of Durkheim's argument which found the cause of religion in crowd gatherings and crowd emotion. He thought that the search for origins was vain, and could only lead to quite untestable speculations. What was observable was an ongoing society in which religious life was clearly important, and in which therefore the function of religion could be clearly established. This function he saw very much in Durkheimian terms: 'Rites can be shown to have a specific social function when, and to the extent that, they have for their effect to regulate, maintain and transmit from one generation to another sentiments on which the constitution of the society depends.'[4] He also accepts Durkheim's view that the relation of men to natural forces has no religious effect except in so far as natural objects are 'objects of important common interests linking together the persons of a community, or are symbolically representative of such objects'. He criticises Frazer for arguing that religious beliefs come into existence through erroneous processes of reasoning, but that having come into existence they have a useful function in ordering society. For Radcliffe-Brown, this function is 'essential and the ultimate reason for their existence'. A further point which Radcliffe-Brown takes from Durkheim, but emphasises even more, is that ritual is the most important aspect of religion, beliefs being secondary. Men may agree on the importance of ritual performances, and on the exact way they should be done, and yet be extremely vague and even inconsistent in their beliefs about gods, spirits and forces. He quotes with approval pre-Confucian and Confucian Chinese philosophers who believed that through sacrifice and religious music the people express and achieve unity, and yet refused to be drawn into metaphysical discussion about the nature of gods and spirits. Thus Radcliffe-Brown thought there should always be a close relation between ritual groups and social structure, but that the nature of the gods addressed in the ritual will be very variable. As worshipper, man is bound by the structure of his society; as myth-maker or theologian he is fancy-free. Radcliffe-Brown quotes with approval a dictum of Whitehead's that 'no account of the uses of symbolism is complete without the recognition that the symbolic elements in life have a tendency to run wild, like vegetation in a tropical forest'.

The likeness and difference of the two modes of approach can be seen in their analyses of totemism. Durkheim saw the clan totem as a sacred symbol of the power and unity of the clan. The fact that the totem was usually an animal or plant used for food resulted from a projection of social relations into external nature. As the tribe was divided into clans, so the natural environment was divided into portions each having a natural affinity with each clan. But the choice of a totem for a particular clan was more or less fortuitous. Radcliffe-Brown saw totemism as dependent on two conditions: (a) hunting and gathering as the only means of getting food and (b) a segmental social structure of moieties, clans, residence and sex groups. Because of the first condition there is a tendency for a ritual attitude to develop towards all plants and animals forming part of the food supply; because of the second, particular segments of the society have a special responsibility for ensuring the supply of food from a particular species, and this is expressed in the totemic rituals, whose aim is to make a particular species of food abundant. The function of totemism in respect of social solidarity is twofold; to express the unity of the totemic group, and to express the relation of the totemic group to the wider whole of the tribe. (Radcliffe-Brown uses Durkheimian terminology in calling these functions contributions to the mechanic and organic solidarity of the tribe respectively.) The ritual attitude to the world of nature is most likely to be developed by primitive people because they tend to interpret all experience in terms of categories drawn from social life, i.e., as the result of the interaction of wills, and do not use a different set of mechanistic categories in dealing with natural phenomena, which are not in any case conceived of as qualitatively distinct from human phenomena. As one of the basic experiences of human life is dependence (here Radcliffe-Brown mentions infantile experience as prototypical), so the ritual attitude extends to natural forces, or rather 'external nature, so-called, comes to be incorporated into the social order as an essential part of it'.

There seems to be a certain ambiguity in Durkheim's and Radcliffe-Brown's ideas about ritual as expressing and maintaining the sense of dependence which is, in their view, essential to an orderly social life. At some points they both seem to believe that man will worship his society, which is necessary to its continuance, only in terms of some symbolism which he himself does not understand. At other points it seems as if ritual could continue even if the symbolism was transparent to the worshipper as well as to the sociologically trained observer, as when Durkheim instances the French Revolution's establishment of the worship of reason, and the growth of religiously flavoured Nationalism. From Radcliffe-Brown's remarks on modern thought as contrasted to primitive thought, it follows that modern men will not have a ritual attitude to objects in nature, but only to social relations and the moral order. Why then should not rituals become a form of conscious dramatisation of the relations of individuals to their society and its traditions? On the contrary, Radcliffe-Brown argues that it is just among modern religions where there is less propitiation of natural forces that there is a tremendous concern about correct religious belief, and groups are created and divided according to such beliefs. Both writers stress the functional necessity of religion to social order, but it is not certain what kinds of belief they would count as essential to religion.

Radcliffe-Brown was more interested than Durkheim in testing his hypotheses by comparative study, and thought he had established a correlation between lineage structure and the worship of ancestral spirits; the latter, he thought, only existed where lineages operated; once these were broken up by social changes, ancestor worship also ceased. This generalisation has been challenged by Evans-Pritchard, who points to examples of ancestral cults in societies without a lineage structure.

Malinowski, a contemporary of Radcliffe-Brown, made the understanding of religion and magic among primitive peoples one of the major themes of his work. From his detailed account of magic and religion among the Trobrianders,[5] a Melanesian people, he was prepared to venture into the field of generalisation. He noticed the importance attributed by the Trobrianders to magical and religious rites, and argued that both arose from emotional stress and anxiety in the face of human weakness. In this respect he is in line with earlier thinkers who saw anxiety as one of the consequences or corollaries of intelligence. Ritual, he thought, could accomplish the transformation of anxiety into confidence. Magic, in his words, 'ritualises optimism', while for religion he makes even bigger claims. 'Religion makes man do the biggest things he is capable of, and it does for man what nothing else can do; it gives him peace and happiness, harmony and a sense of purpose, and it gives all this in an absolute form.'[6] Though he seems to hold to this view of religion as valid for all societies, he believes that religion has other effects than those of enhanced confidence and harmony; it may also provoke conflicts with other groups, and hold back the advance of empirical and scientific knowledge. Though Malinowski asserts a common root to magic and religion, he also sees differences between the two. Religious rites demonstrate and underline social values, social rights and obligations. This expressive and dramatising function he believed essential to the life of any community, and therefore drew pessimistic conclusions from the irreligion of his own day and age. He accepts the functional view of religion expressed by Durkheim, but disagrees with the latter over the negative evaluation of magic as necessarily anti-social. Moreover he attempts to show the significance of particular rites to the individual as well as directly to the society. Thus mortuary rites, to which Malinowski devotes a great deal of attention, are shown as arising partly from each individual's fear of his own death, but also as expressing the conflict of emotions which survivors have towards the dead person, wishing to maintain, yet also to break, the ties, which according to the particular social structure, they have had with him. His view is that funeral rites provide a useful catharsis of the emotions of those most closely affected, and at the same time an expression of the new adjustment of statuses and roles in a group after the death of a member. This is a much more subtle and sociological explanation of funeral rites than the explanation in terms of fear of ghosts offered by Spencer and his school. Religion, then, expresses and helps to continue tradition, and religious rituals are always carried out by, or on behalf of, groups. Magic, on the other hand, is a technique, similar to science in aim, but radically different in form and substance. It may be pursued by groups or individuals. Magic operates in activities where the area of uncertainty is high, and where important social values are involved. Thus Malinowski contrasts the purely common-sense techniques employed by fishers in the safety of the lagoon, with the magic practices surrounding open-sea fishing, where danger and the uncertainty of reward are much greater. In gardening, again, there is much magic employed, and this is related not only to the variability of harvests, but to the fact that a good harvest is not just a necessity against hunger, but a means of fulfilling kinship obligations and of acquiring great social prestige. The emotional impetus towards magical practices may be one of invidious distinction or even of straight hostility; there is black magic as well as white magic. Malinowski believed that magic, as much as religion, was socially conservative in its effect, but since even stable societies have their personal quarrels and structural tensions, so magic and counter-magic will be used in pursuit of conflicting individual interests.

A third important name in the analysis of primitive religion is Evans-Pritchard,[7] whose contribution has been both critical and constructive. First he makes a powerful attack on all those theories of magic and religion which explain them away as fantasy or illusion, even if they emphasise the social usefulness, even necessity, of the illusion. He believes that investigators of primitive religions who hold this point of view do not have the necessary sympathy with those who believe and practise to make a worthwhile analysis of the place of religion in any society. He notes that most convinced positivists have been only armchair anthropologists who have applied criteria of truth drawn from their own culture to quite different systems of thought and action. In particular he criticises the analysis of belief in isolation from practice. A single rite, myth or magic spell, examined on its own, can easily appear as mere irrational fantasy or make-believe. But religious facts should be analysed as a whole, and in relation to other institutional systems of society. They then appear not only as coherent, but 'even critical, sceptical and experimental within the system of beliefs and its idiom'.[8] Rationality in a primitive system of thought and action is of the same kind as in a modern scientific one; it consists of internal consistency of its rules and principles with one another, and their consistency with experience perceived in accordance with these rules. Modern thought analyses experience with different axioms in mind, and therefore structures experience differently. In particular, mechanistic notions of cause and effect are applied more widely, and there is a greater readiness to accept the category of 'chance', whether this is a word which simply admits ignorance and failure to understand an event, or whether this is understood as a word expressing the coming together of an infinitely large number of lines of mechanistic causation to produce a single event. Evans-Pritchard tries to show the reasonableness of a primitive system of thought by analysing religion among the Nuer,[9] and magic and witchcraft among the Azande.[10]

The Nuer are a pastoral people living in the Sudan. Their society is organised in lineages, and is segmentary rather than hierarchical. There is no central authority. It is held together by lineage and affinal ties, which limit the degree to which a dispute can involve the whole society, or divide it into two opposing camps. There is also one clan whose members hereditarily carry the office of 'leopard-skin priests', who are specialised to the function of peacemaking and mediation, and do not bear arms or carry on the blood feud as other lineages and clans may do. In recent times, the Nuer have not been quite isolated but have expanded in one direction to dominate the neighbouring Dinka people, although subject to pressure from the British and Arabs in another direction.

Basic to their religious thinking is the concept of 'spirit'. The word thus translated is used of God, thought of as the creator, unseen, disembodied and universal, but also of a vast range of spirits of the sky and of the lower world, down to fetishes in which the spirit is immanent, but where it is dominated by, rather than dominating, its material home. Evans-Pritchard shows how each group in the society has its 'own' spirit, with whom it is in ritual contact; nevertheless, the unity of spirit as such never entirely disappears in Nuer thinking. (The pattern has resemblances with early Christian and neo-platonist beliefs in the different levels of existence from godhead to brute matter, and with Jewish cabbalism with its doctrine of divine sparks imprisoned in material shells.) This notion of spirit allows for innovations and borrowings without any change in the fundamental principle of the system. For instance, expansion among the neighbouring Dinkas has led to importation of totems, which were conceived as hitherto unknown members of the group—spirits of the lower world. The phenomenon of prophecy, of men declaring that they were possessed by spirits who through them spoke to the people, has arisen only in recent times, in response to foreign contacts. Prophets both led the raids into Dinkaland, and organised and justified the defence against British and Arab authority. But this new role could be accommodated within the pre-existing thought pattern, and Nuer recognised the authority, both of old priests and new prophets.

Evans-Pritchard shows how a very close acquaintance with the people and its language is necessary before the anthropologist can say what the system of religious and magical thinking is. With this close acquaintance many of the apparent illogicalities vanish, though the basic difficulties of maintaining a clear and consistent view of the ways in which a supreme spiritual creator affects the operations of his creation are apparent. But then these basic difficulties have obtained even in the most subtle and sophisticated philosophical and theological thinking. Of two things Evans-Pritchard is quite certain: the first is that 'a structural interpretation explains only certain characteristics of the refractions and not the idea of spirit itself. That idea is broken up by the refracting surface of nature, of society, of culture and of historical experience'.[11] The second is that there is no magical mode of thought operating alongside the 'spirit' mode. The systematising of all experience in terms of spirit, trans-cendant or immanent, seems to make magical thinking unnecessary, and magical practices very few and far between.

This second point provides a link and a contrast with his studies of the Azande, another African people, but this time agricultural in economy, and very hierarchical politically. The whole social structure shows the impress of recent conquest, the royalty and nobility being marked off sharply from the commoners. Among the Azande there is a vague belief in a 'supreme being', occasionally expressed in conversation but never in ritual. There is worship of ancestral spirits at family shrines, but little in the way of religious ceremonial involving the whole, or even substantial segments, of the population. What does occupy a large part in Azande life is magic, revealed in the practices of witchcraft, sorcery, oracular divination and the use of 'medicines'. A witch has the capacity to hurt a man by wishing him ill, without using any physical or verbal means. A sorcerer knows physical means of harming people, and these can be employed in socially approved ways, for example, in order to punish an adulterer, or in socially disapproved ways, enabling an adulterer to get rid of an unwanted husband. Fear of giving a witch cause for ill-will is a substantial motive for keeping the rules of the society and respecting its values, for if a man is generous and neighbourly he will not provoke the witches. If mis-fortune befalls any man then he looks for the cause in terms of witch-beliefs. Who had reason to do him harm? His suspicions can be tested by appealing to oracles and to witch-doctors who provide in their seances a dramatic representation of the battle between good and evil powers acting on men. His answers will be in terms of the network of kinship and local obligations for witch accusations are not random but related to social structure.

The whole complex of beliefs provides an explanatory system for all events, and is a sanction for good behaviour beyond the limits of the family group, within which the authority of the ancestral spirits performs a similar function. The beliefs and practices operate among the commoners, and although nobles and princes may apply to commoners for 'medicines' to increase their power and success, they are always the clients, not the practitioners and specialists. If a commoner aims at becoming powerful by attaching himself to a noble, he uses wealth as his means of social climbing, not magic or religious capacity. There seems a clear distinction between political power and magic or religious roles which is uncommon among primitive peoples.

Evans-Pritchard enquired with great care how far the people distinguished between magic and empirical means. He found that the degree to which magic was added to empirical techniques was very variable, and difficult to interpret in any systematic way. Gong-making had magical practices regularly attached, whereas pot-making did not. The theory of danger and uncertainty being associated with magic did not seem to hold good. The people seemed to distinguish between practices which produced a directly observable result, and those in which some unobservable connection between cause and effect supervened. But in all cases the test of success was applicable, and in their view this test was applicable to all methods equally. Applying that test in their everyday life, the magical means as well as the empirical ones seemed to them justified. There could be recognised failure of one magical means, but the result of this would be to switch to different ones, not to produce scepticism about a whole category of means. To sum up: Evans-Pritchard has effectively described a system of thought and practice in which magic is clearly not derivable from religious practice and belief, in which it is not possible to contrast the unifying function of religion with the disruptive effect of magic, in which religious ritual plays a very small part and religious mythology is very scanty. Whilst there are great differences in social structure and economy between the Azande and the Nuer, and also great differences in their magico-religion, it is impossible to relate these two sets of differences.

This result of two very detailed studies adds weight to Evans-Pritchard's argument that provided the coherence of each system is respected, there is a great need for comparative studies of different societies. The old easy generalisations about primitive religion have been shown up as worthless, and without much comparative research no new ones can ever be established.

Evans-Pritchard's analyses of magic and religion in relation to social structure reveal tension as well as unity, strain as well as harmony, between different groups and roles. Some writers have been especially concerned with ritual expression of these tensions. As one example, I will summarise Gluckman's work on ritual forms of rebellion in some Bantu peoples, particularly the Zulu and Swazi.[12] Among the Zulu, he notes two types of rebellion, the first being the agricultural fertility rituals practised by the women, and addressed to a goddess of fertility. These are exceptional in that only women may carry them out, and men must hide away, thus reversing the normal male predominance in ritual. And the rites themselves largely consist in a reversal of normal sexual roles: the young women dress as men and take charge of the cattle, which is normally forbidden work for them, and their mothers indulge in lewdness and obscenities in direct contradiction to the behaviour normally expected of them. If they come across any men during the ceremonial they attack them, whereas normally women should obey and defer to their menfolk. Thus the goddess is propitiated not by profession of obedience to social norms, but by the direct, if temporary, violation of them.

The second Zulu ritual analysed by Gluckman is the first-fruits ceremony in which the king plays the central role. During this long ritual there are several episodes in which his subjects, particularly the princes of the royal family, express hatred and rejection of royal authority, and in which the king is subject to gruelling and humiliating ordeals. But these rituals Gluckman analyses in terms of catharsis of social tensions necessarily built up in the social structure. In the case of the women the simple inversion of their normal position is obvious; in the case of the king, his family and his subjects, Gluckman stresses the complexity of social relations, not only a straightforward ambivalence towards royal power, which limits as well as saves, but the alliances between king and commoners against royal princes, of princes and commoners against the king, and of the relation of the king to his mother and his wives. All these he believes are dramatised in the ceremonies. There is not just a simple inversion as in the women's ceremonies, but an alternation between songs and dances of threat and rejection, and rituals of exaltation and gratitude to the king as the source of power and success of the whole nation. 'We see that the dramatic, symbolic acting of social relations in their ambivalence is believed to achieve unity and prosperity.'[13] Gluckman believes that such ritual rebellions are only to be found in static, or, as he prefers, 'repetitive' societies, i.e., societies in which while individuals succeed one another, in given statuses, the structure made up of these statuses persists unchanged. There may be quite severe contests to occupy positions of high status, but all concerned accept the values of kinship, sex and seniority, which prescribe the system of differential status. Thus Zulu rules of royal succession never pointed unambiguously to one heir, and rivalries connected with the succession were always lively. But the institution of kingship was accepted by all the rivals as the prize for which they contended.

Gluckman argues that the rituals of rebellion could only find a place in such a repetitive society, but their existence in such a society tends to maintain it and thus to make it more strongly repetitive. Among other examples of ritual dramatisation of the tensions inevitably accompanying a particular social structure may be cited the analysis of female circumcision rites among the Bemba. Dr Richards writes of these, 'they might be regarded as an extreme expression of the dilemma of a matrilineal society in which men are dominant but the line goes through the women'.[14]

As an example of a 'ritual of rebellion' which has vanished with an alteration of social structure I would cite the Nupe rite of initiation in which, so Nadel[15] informs us, young men were subjected to unpleasant ordeals. Now that they can achieve adult independent status outside their kin groups by going out to work and earning money as individuals, they refuse to play their part in these rites which have fallen into disuse. The widespread occurrence of severe initiation rites among primitive peoples has always been interpreted as expressing the tension which must exist between youth and age, but since these rites are not universal, or uniformly severe or elaborate, there must be other structural features which inhibit or exacerbate this necessary tension in human life. This is another question which structural analysis has posed but not yet answered.

Another good example of relational analysis taking account of tensions as well as harmony in social relations is Middleton's account of Lugbara religion.[16] This Ugandan people is composed of clans, sub-clans, lineages and family clusters, and the authority of senior males over their agnatically related juniors is the core institution of their society. The unity of agnatic lineages is expressed ritually in sacrifice to the ancestors, but there is discretion in the elaborateness and frequency of such rituals vested in the lineage head. The ancestors, it is believed, will send sickness to punish those who do not carry out their duties of obedience to elders, abstention from fighting within the group, marital obligations, etc. There is also a belief in witchcraft, which is thought likely to be practised by a man against those of his kin whom he for good or bad reasons envies. While the cult of the ancestors represents a belief in the value of lineage cohesion, the belief in witchcraft recognises that this value is an ideal which is not easy to achieve in practice. Moreover, whilst it is agreed by all that the society is composed of lineages, there is some flexibility as to just which groups of relatives should be recognised as a lineage under one head, whose members should always obey that head. According to the chances of fertility, health and wealth, lineages tend to wax and wane, and the strains in a larger lineage may gradually produce an accepted division into two or more smaller ones. Thus juniors as they grow older tend to struggle for more independence and higher status. If family size and wealth permit, a younger brother or son may try to break away from his elder brother or father and establish a new family cluster. His elders regard this as disloyalty and insubordination which the ancestors will be invoked to punish. On the other hand, the younger man will regard the invocation of the ancestors as a wrongful act of witchcraft interfering with his rights as head of the new lineage. He may invoke the ancestors himself, and if some sickness then afflicts the older man, his claim to the status of lineage or family head is enhanced in the eyes of all. The point is that a society of lineages whose size will wax and wane for many accidental reasons can never be fully repetitive. The inherent conflict between senior and junior is likely to find open expression where some alterations in detail of the structure are attempted within an overall acceptance of lineage seniority as the basis of legitimate authority. This conflict is expressed in religious and magical terms. The rebellion is not in the nature of an occasional saturnalia or reversal of roles, as in Gluckmann's Bantu cases. It is rather a slow process, cropping up now here, now there, in the society, in which ritual can be interpreted either as expressing social values which have come into conflict, or as a means which the actors use in fighting out their battle to retain or to achieve legitimate authority. It is interesting to note that this second interpretation makes of religion a means rather than an end, and modifies the view that religion is purely expressive, as Malinowski and Radcliffe-Brown seem to have believed.

In these detailed studies of cohesion and tension, and the ritual expressions thereof, modern anthropology frequently adverts to the theme of necessary opposition between father and son, between senior and junior kinsmen, or between brothers and kinsmen treated as brothers. Here, it seems, their analysis is not far away from Freudian views of essential conflicts in society. They do not, however, invoke the unconscious and its exaggerated fantasy life to account for rituals connected with these activities, but rather search for those day-to-day routine relations which limit or contribute to rivalry and enmity. Thus it may be argued that land shortage gives rise to more causes of dispute and therefore to more frequent recourse to ritual to express (and perhaps by catharsis to heal) the quarrel. Labour migration, affecting chiefly young men, is bound to alter the structure of relations between old and young, and this will be apparent in ritual terms.

In recent years there has been much study of primitive societies which have been forced to change rapidly because of external pressure, whether from conquerors, administrators, traders or missionaries. Many such societies, though not all, have responded by radical changes in their religious system, and the question has therefore posed itself: under what conditions does this religious response arise? I propose to discuss this question in relation to the known history of the North American Indians subjected to European pressure, and then to raise the possibility of generalisation from this.[17]

New religious movements among the Indians appeared in close correlation with the degree of contact with the Europeans; among the east coast Delaware in the seventeenth century, the Iroquois of the east coast and the great lakes in the eighteenth century, in California after the 1848 gold rush, and in the great plains and western territories in the 1870s and onwards. An American anthropologist, Linton, coined the word 'nativism' to describe these new movements. He chose the word to emphasise that, despite novelty, the point of the cult was to emphasise the worth of Indian traditions and ways of living which the white man's advance was threatening or destroying. The novelty lay in the means by which the cult devotees believed the European threat could be defeated. These means varied, but in all the movements there were two features in common. One was that each movement grew up round a prophet who claimed divine inspiration, often after experience of trances and severe illness; and the other that virtues of self-discipline and sacrifice of self to the common good were preached. Sometimes this was an underlining of traditional virtues, for example, sexual morality, but always there was the new message also, of abstention from alcohol which was demoralising so many Indians. One of the best documented examples of 'nativism' was the Ghost Dance cult which spread widely among the Plains Indians in two waves, in the 1870s and 1890s, but had earlier smaller manifestations. It attracted tribes, rather than individuals, though not all who came into contact with it were affected, and its great hope was to bring back the glorious past age of the Indians. The devotees refused to contemplate any adaptation of their hunting culture to the new situation, agricultural techniques being looked on as sacrilege. The central belief was that by complete obedience to traditional norms, and by the repeated performance of a modified traditional dance, the dead ancestors would return to chase the Europeans away and bring back the buffalo on which the old way of life depended. Some believers thought that the dance gave them immunity to European bullets.

The cult brought its devotees into conflict with white authority, and partly because of military defeats and the outlawing of the cult, it faded away in the 1890s. It was succeeded, among many of the same tribes, by the Peyote cult. This also had many variants, according to the detail of the vision of each prophet. But in all its variants it was less 'nativist' than the Ghost Dance, because Christian elements always played some part, and because the eating of peyote was given a quite new significance. The essential element of the ritual was the sacramental eating of part of the peyote plant, which had been known and used traditionally as a means of inducing trances and hallucinations which were thought to cure disease. The new cult gave this belief in a way of healing individual illnesses a collective interpretation. When all Indians had come to practise the cult their social redemption would be achieved. In spite of differences in detail among the different Peyote groups, and even rivalries among their leaders, the pan-Indian aspect of the cult was strongly marked. As such it roused the opposition of traditional shamans and medicine men, and also the suspicion of missionaries and government officials, who saw it as a corruption of Christianity and as a narcotic addiction which would be as damaging as the alcoholism against which it fought. The tendency for the Peyote groups to amalgamate and organise on a national basis was probably strengthened by this government opposition. The white man's techniques of organisation and pressure for legal change were effectively learned, and the governmental opposition, whilst severe, was moderated by the fact that Peyote groups never used military means, and did not look forward to a sudden reversal of white and Indian positions, but rather to a future in which Indians could live in dignity and self-respect alongside the whites. Two large Peyote churches eventually came into recognised existence and persist to this day. It is clear that the Ghost Dance and Peyote represent on the one hand a more hostile, and on the other a more adaptive response to European pressure. One sought to restore in detail an old culture; the other looks forward to a new one whose detail cannot be prescribed in advance. One relies entirely on Indian beliefs and practices; the other contains a large admixture of foreign elements which nevertheless were used in support of Indian aspirations and identity.

A third kind of response to European contact is exemplified in the Great Message cult, which began during the period of the American revolutionary war of 1776–82 and continues to this day. Its leaders, whilst claiming direct inspiration from God, were tribal chiefs, whilst the leaders of the Ghost Dance and Peyote cults were, typically, individuals who had no traditional authority within the tribe. Its greatest leaders were Iroquois chiefs who had friendly and close relations with Quaker and Moravian settlements, and many elements in the Great Message show the influence of these peaceable representatives of Christianity. It should also be remembered that the Iroquois formed a powerful federation of tribes who were courted as allies by British, French and American leaders. Thus, though partially disorganised by disease, alcoholism and imprudent sale of tribal lands, they were not completely powerless, *vis-à-vis* the new settlers. This factor no doubt also helped to shape the Great Message, which proclaimed the separate destiny which God had for the Indians, but preached peace with the whites, and the adoption of their educational and farming techniques, the refusal to sell land to them, and the usual elements of tribal self-discipline and temperance. The after-life of heaven and hell was invoked as sanction for these moral commands, but there was no vision of a sudden creation, or re-creation, of a perfect society on this earth. In terms of ritual and mythology, the Great Message proclaimed the identity of the Christian God with the Iroquois 'Great Spirit', and swept many of the traditional dances and festivals away, retaining a simplified seasonal cycle with a somewhat Christianised interpretation. Since the spread of the Great Message coincided with a demographic revival among the Iroquois, and with their adoption of economic techniques useful to survival in the new circumstances, it has been looked on as the means by which this apparently necessary adaptation was achieved. Even accepting this interpretation, it is a difficult question as to how much deliberate social purpose was involved. It is relevant to note that not all the Iroquois, let alone other tribes, adopted the cult. That part of the federation which came under Catholic influence never adopted the Message. And among those who did there was a split in 1820 between those who were satisfied with the original version, and those who went on to adopt a greater part of orthodox Christian doctrine and ritual. Thus this apparently very adaptive cult did not maintain either the old unity of the Iroquois or the new unity which the followers originally created for themselves. It is also worth mentioning that the collective or moral aspects of the cult were sometimes subordinate to its use as a magical means of healing individual ills.

These three examples from North America indicate that the response to severe external pressure may be predominantly apocalyptic as in the Ghost Dance; actively moralising and reformist as in the Great Message; or passive and mystical as in the Peyote cult. (As I mentioned earlier, despite these different emphases, all three exhorted their followers to adopt a morality of self-discipline as the basis of their struggle.) These three kinds of religious response could be matched in African, Melanesian, Polynesian and Asian settings. Few would be found so purely 'nativistic' as the Ghost Dances, but an enormous number and variety of syncretistic cults could be listed, showing borrowing not only of Christian elements, but of Moslem, Hindu and Buddhist ones. However hostile the cult may be to the conqueror, it usually has borrowed something in myth or ritual from the conqueror's religion. Of course, such borrowing also goes on when contact between societies is on a more equal basis; the point I wish to make is that it is not prevented by resentment or hostility. There is frequently an identification of Jehovah or Allah, or one of the great Gods of Hinduism, with the indigenous high God or supreme spirit. Those peoples who have been encouraged by Protestant missions to read the Old Testament as well as the New have sometimes seen themselves as another 'chosen people' with a direct and unique relation with God, whilst it has always been easy to identify a new religious leader with the Messiah, or with Christ returned to earth, or with the 'hidden imam' of heretical Islamic sects.

Close inspection of the vast number of these 'religions of the oppressed'[18] reveals the difficulty of generalising about their origin, the course they run, or their effectiveness in throwing off foreign domination. The last question has given rise to much argument about the rationality of these cults, with the familiar difficulty of judging the matter from inside rather than outside the culture, and not invoking the benefit of hindsight. Some points, however, may be stated confidently. First, religious movements believing in some sudden achievement of an earthly paradise by ritual means are not confined to societies which have suffered the cultural shock of foreign invasion or economic exploitation. Pereira de Queiroz,[19] the expert on messianic cults in Brazil, records instances of Indian peoples coming from the interior to the coast with a belief that by fasting and dancing they will be able to fly over the ocean to a land without evil. These peoples had had no contact whatever with Spanish or Portuguese conquerors. Some investigators of the messianic cults in the Congo believe that they began before the European impact was felt, though later cults have had a strongly European flavour.

Second, a severe cultural shock does not necessarily result in a new or radically altered religion expressing hostility against the invader or aiming to restore the previous state of affairs. We have seen that some American Indian tribes did not take up the Ghost Dance or any alternative cult. The Australian aborigines suffered great disruption of their way of living, but developed no religious protest against it, whereas their neighbours on the Melanesian islands have originated a succession of apocalyptic and anti-European movements.

Thirdly, it is not possible to argue that, if there is a reaction of defiance and protest against the invader, it will first take a religious form, proclaiming some supernatural means of restoring independence, and that after successive disappointments of such movements it will take a non-religious political form more adapted to the realities of the situation. Peter Worsley, in his book on the Melanesian cargo cults, has traced this sequence for that particular region, but it is not possible to generalise it. The example of the Great Message shows that a realistic kind of adaptation may be preached at the very beginning of the reaction to the outsider, not after the failure of apocalyptic movements. It also shows that a religious message can be as realistic and adaptive as a political one. African experience is also relevant here, for it suggests that the sequence may be from politics to religion as well as from religion to politics. Simon Matswa, a member of the Bakongo people, who lived in France in the 1920s, organised his fellow tribesmen in France to influence French colonial policy, and to improve the lot of the Bakongo at home by beginning *les amicales*, a sort of friendly society movement. He was imprisoned by the French government, and subsequently became a hero to his followers, who began to identify him with Christ. After his death they came to believe that he would return and liberate his people. Pilgrimages began, and a cult developed. In this case, it appears as if the followers almost forced divinity on a secular leader. The rise of the Mau-Mau in Kenya is also interesting, because here the magico-religious practices seem to have been grafted on to the original political protest movement as a deliberate tactic to strengthen its following in numbers and devotion. In this it was highly successful.

It is also not always the case that religions of protest are effective in bringing together peoples in larger organisations, acting as the forerunner of Nationalism. This is partly borne out by the Melanesian and North American Indian experiences, but less so by African, South American and Asian examples. The fragmentation of Bantu churches in Africa is well known, and the 'cities of God' which have formed around renegade Catholic priests in South American communities do not seem to play any role in widening the Indian outlook to a more national one. The very marked tendency for religions of protest to take shape around a prophetic leader means that the likelihood of their embracing great numbers of people without schism is low. It may well be that the leader draws people as individuals rather than as members of traditional groups such as tribes, though here the variations are enormous. But even if his appeal is not limited to traditional groups of tribes or villages, it is not necessarily answered on such a scale as to produce something like a nationalist movement.

The same point may be made by inspecting the very diverse ways in which an alien culture or ruler can dominate a primitive one. Are there only traders or are there also immigrants? If the latter, do they come gradually or in sudden rushes? Is one colonial power or Christian mission established, or are there changes between British, German and Japanese, or rivalries between Catholic and Protestant? Is the indigenous people already divided into classes, or is it relatively egalitarian and homogeneous in culture? When these and similar questions are answered, it is not surprising to find that religions of protest often take root in only a part of the group subjected to alien influence and rule. Thus the anti-British Hau-Hau movement among the Maori left many tribes untouched, for these latter saw the British as inoffensive, even useful in imposing peace on a war-torn land, rather than as robbers of tribal territory. There were powerful syncretistic cults which rebelled against mission Christianity in Hawaii and Tahiti, but they had to fight against their own convert-kings, as well as against the foreigners. Mair stresses the instrumental as well as the expressive character of religion when she writes 'when converts have destroyed their cult objects in obedience to mission instructions, they have not been renouncing error, still less repenting sin, but formally transferring their allegiance from the less powerful to the more powerful spirit'.[20] The success of missions is as striking as the resentment against them.

These observations have some relevance to theories of religion such as Durkheim's, Radcliffe-Brown's or Malinowski's. If the stranger's god can be substituted for, or identified with, the native god, can the latter be only a symbol of the power of an ongoing society over its individual members? If religion safeguards each society from selfishness and despair, why have some primitive peoples shown no effective religious reply to external threat, and allowed themselves to be completely demoralised by the impact of European intruders on their traditional culture?

Functional analyses of stable primitive societies assume that religion has a power to preserve and invigorate a given society. Investigation of cases of rapid social change show a more complicated picture. In these cases, religion appears not as a means of defending the old, but of changing it. Converts to the alien's religion necessarily weaken traditional social structure. For instance, they may refuse to follow traditional marriage patterns involving transfer of bride-wealth, and thus attack kinship structure at a vital point. Or they may opt out of traditional judicial institutions because these involve acknowledgement of 'false gods'. Converts to a religion of protest disrupt tradition by following new leaders rather than priests. These phenomena are inconsistent with Durkheim's main theory, and also with Radcliffe-Brown's ideas that religion expresses a sense of dependence, if this is taken to be a sense of dependence on the particular society in which an individual has grown up. If it is to be taken only as a name for some innate tendency to defer to whatever seems the most powerful authority at a given moment, regardless of previous social loyalties, then this is a psychological generalisation which may well be true (Freud would certainly think so), but cannot explain both conservative and revolutionary and innovating religion. Studies of social change throw light on the limits of the supposed power of existing religions to strengthen traditional loyalties and structure. Why should it in some contexts seem so strong, in others so weak? Clearly there is a need for comparative studies to test functional hypotheses, both in order to try to answer this kind of question, and in order to understand the variable importance of ritual, witchcraft, and other magico-religious phenomena in different societies. There is clearly no simple connection between magic and technology, or between centralised political power and the attribution of sacred qualities to that power. It may well appear that functional hypotheses on their own will always be inadequate to account for the range of phenomena, and that historical data are also required.

Among other items of unfinished business among anthropologists is the study of styles of thought, the relation between empirical and symbolic, instrumental and expressive modes. One of the leading figures here is Lévi-Strauss who advocates an approach from the side of linguistics as well as from the side of social structure. He is concerned with structures of human thought, and the resemblance between social expression of feeling in myth or ritual, and the individual's discharge of emotion in recapitulating his own life-history, as in the psychoanalytic situation. Here again we seem to come near to the view of religion as a kind of drama. But the issues Lévi-Strauss raises, although based on his study of anthropological material, go beyond that, and are equally relevant to the understanding of religion in complex societies also.

1. H. Hubert and M. Mauss, 'Sketch of a General Theory of Magic', *Année Sociologique*, 1902.

2. H. Hubert and M. Mauss, *Mélanges d'Histoire des Réligions*, 1909.

3. J. E. Harrison, *Ancient Art and Ritual*, 1913.
   —*Prolegomena to the Study of Greek Religion,* 1922.

4. This and subsequent quotations in this paragraph are all from the article '*Religion and Society*' by A. Radcliffe-Brown, *Journal of the Royal Anthropological Institute*, vol. LXXV, 1945.

5. B. Malinowski, *Argonauts of the Western Pacific*, 1932.
   —*Coral Gardens and their Magic*, 1935.
   —*Magic, Science and Religion*, 1948.

6. B. Malinowski, *Science and Religion: A Symposium*, Ed. by J. Huxley, 1931.

7. E. Evans-Pritchard, *Theories of Primitive Religion*, 1965.

8. ibid., p. 29.

9. E. Evans-Pritchard, *Nuer Religion*, 1956.

10. E. Evans-Pritchard, *Witchcraft, Oracles and Magic among the Azande*, 1937.

11. E. Evans-Pritchard, *Nuer Religion*, p. 121.

12. M. Gluckman, *Rituals of Rebellion in S.E. Africa*, 1954.

13. ibid., p. 19.

14. A. I. Richards, *Chisungu*, 1956, p. 159.

15. S. F. Nadel, *Nupe Religion*, 1954.

16. J. Middleton, *Lugbara Religion*, 1964.

17. E. Norbeck, *Religion in Primitive Society*, 1961, ch. 13.

18. A comprehensive catalogue is to be found in V. Lanternari, *Religions of the Oppressed*, trans. by L. Sergio, 1963.

19. Pereira de Queiroz, 'Messianic Movements in Brazil', *Archives de Sociologie des Réligions*, 1958.

20. L. Mair, *New Nations*, 1963, p. 175.

4

FUNCTIONAL THEORIES OF RELIGION

Many writers since his day have reasserted Durkheim's view that the social function of religion is to support and conserve an ongoing society. Religion, they say, is functional to social cohesion and solidarity. On the other hand, these post-Durkheimian scholars, with the partial exception of Radcliffe-Brown, have been uniformly critical of Durkheim's analysis of the causes of religious faith, refusing to accept his view that it arises out of heightened sociability and suggestibility in a crowd situation. These critics who wish to retain the function, but to dispense with the cause, have therefore to find some other root of religion, if they are not to fall back on a circular argument that since society needs religion for its cohesion and solidarity, somehow religion arises to meet the supposed need. I would like to examine some functional theories which try to avoid this trap of circularity, and see how they conceive of religion as arising from basic human needs and predicaments. I propose to refer to the American writers Yinger,[1] O'Dea,[2] Berger[3] and Luckmann,[4] and to compare their views with those of Marx and Freud, both of whom also stressed the functional necessity of religion in most, though not all, human societies.

A feature common to the group of American scholars is the insistence that religious belief and ritual, being universal, can only be explained by equally universal qualities of human life, individual or social. They all agree in rejecting the old positivist view that religion arises in particular conditions of ignorance and intellectual inadequacy which will not last for ever. They wish to show how certain essential attributes of humanity must issue in religious phenomena, and in attempting to do this they suggest that religions function to support social values and rules.

Yinger's main point is that all men need some absolute values to live by, and that these must provide an answer to the ultimate problems of life and death. Religions answer to this need, whereas no amount of empirical knowledge or development of science can do so. In fact scientific development now includes a deliberate examination of the methods and scope of science which brings to light its limitations in answering human anxieties and frustrations. Yinger accepts, however, that in modern societies there are apparently irreligious people who do not profess any creed or join in any ritual. In his view, nevertheless, they all have some absolute value to keep them going, and he identifies such various ones as devotion to the scientific pursuit of truth, absolute loyalty to a gang, and enormous enthusiasm for poker! But these values are only partially functional equivalents to religion because they give no answer to the question of meaning and purpose as it arises at the crises of life. Since all men must face death, and usually other grave frustrations as well, religion in its full sense is necessary to them. He admits that there are those who have a faith in science which leads them to deny any need for religion or trust in its answers, but he argues that those who proclaim that they need no value beyond that of scientific truth in fact have an unverifiable faith in the power of science to answer questions of values. By his definition, they are religious in spite of themselves.

So far his argument rests on straightforward statements about human nature, without reference to particular kinds of social structure. However, in his book *Sociology Looks at Religion* he seems to rely partly on a somewhat different and rather Durkheimian argument, which involves looking at the specific qualities of particular groups. In the USA today, he says, religious groups are pre-eminently those in which members may find a stable identity in a set of enduring interpersonal relations. Relationships of this satisfying kind are not to be found in other areas of American life, where impersonal, instrumental and transitory relations are dominant. He does not go so far as to say that a particular faith in God grows out of the satisfactions of participating in such a group, but he does strongly imply that a religious answer to ultimate problems of value and purpose carries more weight with the individual because of such participation. If we take this argument in conjunction with the one asserting a human generic need for religion, a problem arises. It seems that particular religions are to be seen as a compound of group loyalties expressed symbolically, and answers to ethical and metaphysical problems posed by individuals. Loyalty to the group enables the religious answer to these problems to carry conviction. But if this is so, and particularly if it is participation in relatively small interpersonal groups which best fortifies religious conviction, the function of providing personal reassurance, and the function of contributing to social solidarity may be in conflict. It is not clear why a religion which meets the personal need for ultimate meaning in the face of death and frustration should also constitute 'a refusal to allow hostility to tear apart one's human associations'.[5] In fact if it is pre-eminently small group life which fosters religious conviction, the likelihood of a clash between congregational religion and social order within a large group such as a modern state is quite obvious. Thus Christian sects have inspired immense faith and enthusiasm in their members, but this may coexist with withdrawal from, or even hostility to, the wider society within which the sect grows up. At the level of personal religious leadership, the point may be illustrated by reference to Mohammed, Calvin and Loyola. Each of these was clearly integrated and inspired as a person by his particular religious faith. Yet in each of these cases, and many others could be added, the very source of personal reassurance was a reason for extreme hostility to others outside the Faith. Of course, it may well be said that religious faith subdues hostilities arising within the group of the faithful, but this is true of any kind of group loyalty to any kind of group. Yinger clearly does not want to be thoroughly Durkheimian, and simply equate religious beliefs with belief in symbols of social loyalty. He wishes to hold on to the differentiating aspect of religious belief, which to him is its provision of answers to ultimate questions transcending the life and goals of particular groups, but in so doing he shows how the social function which he has asserted as basic to religion may not in fact be fulfilled. So far as he emphasises personal need for reassurance he is able to give an account of prophetic and innovating religion which Durkheimian theory cannot achieve without self-destructive qualifications. His account also permits him to examine the strength and weakness of the integrative function of religion in different kinds of social structures. He concludes that a society is always tending 'to recover or discover a unifying religious theme',[6] which suggests that it is experience of and in a particular society which allows men to construct religious barriers against despair and frustration. In a word, Yinger states an individual and a social 'need' for religion, but hardly succeeds in systematically relating the one to the other. In so doing he tends to overlook the cases of social divisiveness of religious belief, such as the wars of religion in sixteenth- and seventeenth-century Europe.

Berger's work in the sociology of religion is more recent; his theory is fully set out in *The Social Reality of Religion* published in 1969. He shares many ideas with his colleague Luckmann, author of *The Invisible Religion*, appearing in 1963 (English translation in 1967). Both theorists begin from the position that men, being intelligent, social and capable of using language, are never content with raw experience, but try to build from it a 'system of meanings'. Experience is structured in relation to goals, desires and memories, in a way which makes each item consistent with all others in an overall pattern. This system of meanings is a social, not an individual, product, a product of all men living in interrelation at any one time, and of their forbears too. It therefore seems to each individual to have an objective existence outside him. Each contributes something, but the whole is extra-individual and 'socially objectivated'. This 'system of meanings', however, can only persist if it continues to be supported by experience, and new items interpreted consistently with the general pattern. Hence at this point in the discussion Berger introduces the notion that each 'system of meanings' depends on a 'plausibility structure'. But he warns that his view should not be taken in any way as equivalent to a statement that religion is always an epiphenomenon of social structure, as merely a kind of rationalisation or dramatisation of everyday secular activities. On the contrary, he argues in respect of the 'collapse of plausibility suffered by religion in the contemporary situation', that to a large extent 'Christianity has been its own gravedigger', that is, the way Christianity defines the relation of men to their church and society has been one important fact in a process of objective (i.e., structural) and subjective secularisation in hitherto Christian societies. He argues that there is a reciprocal influence between systems of meaning, which include religious systems, and the social and personal experience which men try to interpret in the light of such systems.

Berger repeatedly refers to the human terror of chaos, the fear of confronting, without a comprehensive framework of interpretation, the flux of experience. He believes there is in us an innate horror of meaninglessness, so that men cling to socially objectivated systems of meaning. While these essential supports of human life are social, it is also true that the degree to which any one support will appeal to a number of people, will depend to a great extent on the similarity or diversity of their experience. Thus Berger explains the religious pluralism of present-day America in terms not only of secularising tendencies within Christianity itself, for example its readiness to withdraw from control of economic life, and its admission of the independent realm of science, but also of the diversity of social roles in large-scale industrial society. This diversity makes for very different kinds of 'plausibility structure', therefore there are many different religious tastes to be catered for. Given the degree of religious pluralism in the USA today, the religious specialists are forced away from their old role of authoritatively handing down traditional systems of meaning. They become more and more like sellers competing in a market place to meet a variety of demands. The demand is always there, because religious belief is functionally necessary to individuals. Yet it cannot become completely individualised since every religious system stems from the continuous social enterprise of interpreting and re-interpreting experience. But in diversified societies there will be many competing, though not necessarily antagonistic, interpretations, each of which tends to suit a relatively small group of 'consumers'. The 'producers' contend with each other in a market-like situation.

If Berger's view is true, it appears that the function of religion in strengthening and engendering social solidarity is fundamentally weakened in modern American society. His statement that 'religion has been one of the most effective bulwarks against anomie throughout human history',[7] can be true only to the extent individuals are enabled to hold more confidently to the rules and values of their particular religious group. Religious belief would not check anomie in relation to the values and rules of the larger social units, such as nation or class, unless the various religious groups which together comprise the membership of class or nation are all proclaiming the same set of values. That they do in fact do this is the view of Herberg[8] and Wilson,[9] who describe all the contemporary American religious groups (bar a few insignificant sects) as having the same moral values, the sanctification of 'the American way of life'. But, logically enough, they agree from this observation that they expect denominational boundaries to be more and more blurred, and ecumenism to grow in strength, whereas Berger contends that religious pluralism will continue because of diversity of experience. Herberg's observation about the common content of nearly all American religious groups might be reconciled with Berger's thesis by pressing a little further the latter's market analogy. Perhaps he would accept that only the 'packaging' of the religious content differs from one denomination to another, responding to the slight difference in consumer preference, arising from diversity of experience, among the whole body of religious 'consumers' in the USA. This, however, is very doubtful, for both Berger and his colleague Luckmann suspect that in the USA today any form of patriotic religion rings false, and that there is not the widespread satisfaction with current experience of the American way of life that would make an effective 'plausibility structure' for such a religion. In general Berger holds to a dialectical relation between social structure and religion; in particular he argues that the complex and changing social structure of the USA generates dissatisfaction with traditional faiths, and the substitution of many small religious groups proclaiming systems of meaning different from the traditional ones and different from one another. If the persistence of the larger whole, the American society, demonstrates that its members show some degree of social solidarity, this, by Berger's argument, would seem to occur without benefit of religion.

His analysis raises again the question of the religious quality of such movements as Nationalism and Communism. From Berger's account of how systems of meaning grow, and how their apex is always religious, it seems that such political movements, whenever they proclaim absolute values and inevitable historical processes, must be deemed religious. Yet their occurrence in large-scale complex societies goes against his view that diversity of experience in such societies makes for religious pluralism, for the whole effect of such movements is to deny the validity of other systems of meaning. Berger views these movements as regressive and ephemeral, just as he seems to view traditional Christianity with its acceptance of the American way of life, as weak and residual. It appears that the future lies with new or radically altered religions. Yet some of the political religions have lasted longer than many of the new sects and cults in the USA. Soviet and Chinese Communism seem to have considerable vitality, and German Nationalism of the most extreme and ritualistic kind was only ended by defeat at the hand of foreign armies. Berger's theory requires that these movements should be ephemeral and unsuccessful, but it is not clear to me that they are.

Luckmann's recent book, *The Invisible Religion*, again tries to account for the weakness of institutional religion in the modern Western world, while holding to a view of man's nature which makes him fundamentally religious. Hence the choice of title. The author's description of systems of ideas, or world-views, being at one and the same time social products external to the individual, yet always subject to criticism or confirmation by individual experience, is the same as Berger's. He concludes thus: 'It is in keeping with an elementary sense of the concept of religion to call the transcendence of biological nature by the human organism a religious phenomenon. As we have tried to show, this phenomenon rests upon the functional relation of self and society. We may, therefore, regard the social processes that lead to the formation of self as fundamentally religious. . . . In showing the religious quality of the social processes by which consciousness and conscience are individuated we identified the universal yet specific anthropological condition of religion.'[10] Yet he is interested to isolate the conditions which underlie religion in the narrower sense of belief in a 'sacred cosmos'. This sacred cosmos is marked off by the generality of its concepts, by mystery deriving from its transcendence of an everyday world explicable in less general terms, and by the use of symbols, for example, in ritual. The remainder of the system of ideas or world-view, while linked with and in a sense validated by the over-arching sacred cosmos, constitutes the secular or profane sphere. Religion in this narrower sense, as well as in the wider one insisted on in the definition, is universal. What is not universal is its embodiment in institutions. Institutionalisation, in Luckmann's view, depends on three conditions: first, that there exists an economic surplus permitting the support of religious specialists; second, that contact with other societies occurs, leading a society to greater awareness of its own sacred cosmos, and to greater readiness to articulate and defend it; third, that the religious specialists develop a vested interest in the elaboration and defence of their particular system. However, institutional specialisation of religion carries with it the risk of making the ideas constituting the sacred cosmos less responsive to the ongoing experience of the laity, the non-specialists. Thus religion may tend to become 'for Sundays only' and in Luckmann's view this is the position to which the traditional faiths have been reduced in the Western world. Yet, invisibly, men are and must continue to be religious, because they strive for a general system of interpretation of experience, and because they seek answers to questions of ultimate purpose. As religious specialists have been institutionally differentiated, so also have a range of other institutions been differentiated, for instance, political, judicial, economic, cultural. Each tends to develop its own set of secular norms, to develop and guard a degree of autonomy. The specialists of the old traditional sacred cosmos, the priests and theologians, have been unable, according to Luckmann, to moralise these secular and autonomous norms by bringing them into correspondence with the more general precepts of the sacred order, and this failure is one of the reasons for their current weakness. But new religions, as they emerge from invisibility, will be faced with the same task. Should one or the other succeed, it will again be faced with the same risks consequent upon institutionalisation which have been traced in the history of Christianity in the Western world. Thus Luckmann puts forward his own version of the dialectic between religion and social structure, and suggests reasons why religion may sometimes be functional to a given society, and sometimes dysfunctional. His conclusion seems to entail that in a static society, 'visible', i.e., institutionalised, religion will always be functional for socialn cohesion, but that the more quickly society changes, the more variable will be the function of institutionalised religion, and the more likely that alongside it will exist kinds of religious belief not yet institutionalised.

O'Dea puts forward yet a fourth analysis of religion in functional terms. Like Yinger he argues that the emotions man experiences at the 'breaking-points of contingency, powerlessness and scarcity' are the raw material of religion. Unlike Yinger, however, O'Dea concedes that there may also be a non-religious response to these situations: 'whereas the religious man affirms a "something more", the non-religious man sees simply a "nothing else".'[11] Nevertheless he accepts that the religious answer has been practically universal, and has been incorporated into institutional beliefs and practices. 'Established religion, by institutionalising answers and mechanisms of adjustment at the limit-situation—a breaking-point involving ultimacy—is able to perform the functions in support of social stability and personal adjustment indicated by functional theory'.[12] O'Dea breaks down these functions into five components, four of which relate to personal adjustment and identity, and one to social control by 'sacralising social norms'. But he also specifies a positive function of prophetic, i.e., innovating, as against established religion; this function, he says, is the criticism of established norms to facilitate a better adjustment of the social structure to new circumstances. Alongside his list of the ways in which religion, established or prophetic, can be functional to society, he sets a list of possible dysfunctions, and these are interesting in showing that the dysfunctions occur in respect of personal and structural adaptation to change, i.e., they would not be dysfunctions in a quite static society. Predictably there is some overlap between O'Dea's dysfunctional aspects of religion, and the ideas of Berger and Luckmann on the reason for the contemporary weakness of religious faiths. For instance, O'Dea argues that a religion which 'ritualises optimism' too strongly may inhibit protest against injustice and unnecessary sufferings, and that a religion which 'sacralises social norms' may prevent the adaptation of rules to new circumstances. Berger and Luckmann contend similarly that the rigidities of institutionalised religion open a gap, unless static conditions prevail, between the meanings handed down by tradition and the meanings verified in the ongoing subjective experience of society's members.

O'Dea's dysfunction of prophetic religion, that it can be Utopian and intolerant, seems a useful reminder of the nature of some prophetic religions, though intolerance need not be dysfunctional for the group of believers, and whether Utopianism is functional or dysfunctional for that group would need much more discussion than O'Dea gives it. But his pin-pointing of these characteristics of some prophetic religions does show up a certain vagueness in the ideas of Berger and Luckmann on how a new 'sacred cosmos', more congruent with current experience, may be built up. Do they believe that a new religion will be in some way more realistic, for example, that it will not contain dogmas that contradict the world picture of science; or is it equally possible for a new religion to use any kind of fantasy provided only that it chimes in with the current discontents and goals of a group? Are the Black Muslims, Scientology, and ultra-liberal Protestantism all equally explicable in terms of the refashioning of world-views in greater congruence with current experience?

O'Dea agrees with Berger, Luckmann and Yinger that the relation of religion to social structure is a dialectical one. He has no overall theory of this dialectical relation, but his list of possible functions and dysfunctions of established and prophetic religions seems a reasonable starting-point for a detailed exploration of the issue. It is to my mind another advantage of his approach that he retains a sense of the difference between religious and scientific categories of interpretation of experience, and admits at least the possibility that some men will be satisfied with the second category. When Luckmann associates generality, mystery and symbolism as the three essential differentia of the 'sacred cosmos' he seems to merge science, religion and art together, rather than provide criteria for distinguishing them, although he clearly wishes to treat religion as a separable category. The dimension missing in his conception of the 'sacred cosmos' is that of power. As the phenomenological approach to religion has taught us, and as a study of ritual very quickly confirms, religion is concerned with the power of the sacred over men, the duty of men to conform their will to God's, the possibility of affecting the operations of sacred power by prayer and sacrifice. Mystery and symbol are there, not by virtue of their association with concepts of the greatest generality, but by their association with the propitiation and understanding of a sacred power whose nature is not fully revealed, and which can therefore only be approached through symbols.

If this aspect of the sacred as power is glossed over, we have in the ideas of Berger and Luckmann simply a sociological theory of knowledge which shows that men cannot but build 'socially objectivated systems of meaning'. But it leaves in the air the question of why a qualitatively different 'sacred cosmos' should form the apex of each system, and whether it will function to support any particular social order. On the other hand, if the aspect of the sacred as power is stressed, the grounds of belief in such a power seem to be only that it is part of a system of meanings which is external to the individual, since such a system can only be produced by the interaction of men in space and time. But this is simply a revival of the Durkheimian conception of the power of the social over the individual, a revival which carries with it the old difficulty that if the sacred equals the social, and all ideas are the product of social life, there is nothing left to go into the profane sphere, and everything is deemed religious. Now men may believe in the law of gravity and the existence of a loving God, but only God is worshipped. The difference of attitude to each idea cannot be elucidated in terms of the social origins of all ideas. Our authors have interesting things to say about the interaction of systems of ideas and social structures in modern industrial societies, and therefore about the function or dysfunction of these ideas in respect of the cohesion of various social groups such as family and state; what they do not show is that religious ideas have a necessarily stronger role to play in the maintenance of social groups than other kinds of ideas. Religion, at least in the modern world, appears as functional to individuals rather than to social wholes, and as a provider of explanations rather than a source and sanction of obligation.

The functional theories of Marx and Freud are at least clear on this score; each tries to discover the source of that obligation to a sacred power which lies at the heart of religion. As we shall see, Marx finds it in social inequality, Freud in the bio-social pattern of the human family.

Marx was not primarily interested in religion, and his works contain only general references to it. But it was he who put forward a framework of ideas,[13] which Engels used to analyse particular aspects of religious history. Engels wrote at some length on early Christianity[14] and the class structure of the society within which it grew, on the religious aspects of the German Peasants' War of the sixteenth century,[15] and on the apparent irreligion of the nineteenth-century English working class.[16]

Marx's theory of religion is part of his general theory of alienation. Men in their life together, he argues, create social products. These may be material objects, such as food and buildings, or immaterial products, such as a structure of social rules, a science or a religion. So long as men are not divided into opposing classes, as they were not during the stage of primitive Communism, these social products are recognised as having been fashioned by men, and therefore capable of being refashioned by them. But so soon as class divisions occur, their first form being that of a slave-owning society, alienation sets in. That is, each individual begins to conceive the products of his society as part of a reality quite external to him, which he cannot control, and to which he must submit. In submitting, whether it be to the loss of his control over material goods which he has helped to create, to the political order, or to religious commandments, a man loses his true humanity, and loses touch with the real world, for he can only understand the world by getting to grips with it and trying to control it. Religious belief, the acceptance of particular dogmas and particular codes of behaviour as absolutely and ultimately true, is more typical of the exploited class than of their oppressors; their lack of property, and therefore of command over the circumstances of their lives, is reflected in their religious submissiveness. Their faith legitimates for them the economic and political order which keeps them in subjection, and offers them compensation for their deprivations in fantasies of an after-life. Marx and Engels were not so clear as to why the ruling class of an epoch should be alienated in terms of religious faith, why they, like their subjects, should believe that the social order they dominated was God-given and not a human creation. Partly their answer is to deny that the ruling class is truly religious, to argue that it sees through the religion that it practises, and practises it only to keep the essential faith alive in the lower orders. Examples are culled from history to show that rulers have recognised their faith to be a means of maintaining an unequal social order, and the inference is drawn that though they deceived others, they were undeceived. Apt quotations to this effect are drawn from Machiavelli, Voltaire and Napoleon. Yet sometimes it is implied that the ruling classes could themselves also be alienated; in trying to maintain their privileged position they were bound to come to such a distorted view of human capacities and creativity as to believe that the social order depended on a divine and unques-

tionable authority. Finally, since Marx realised that primitive as
well as class-ridden societies, were religious, he argues that the
source of these truly primitive religions lies in the primitives' ignorance of natural processes, and the consequent emotions of dependence
and fear of natural forces. While this ignorance persists in any
degree, there will be occasions when the need to deify and propitiate
natural forces is overwhelming, and these would revitalise the
religious outlook in all classes. But Marx is not much concerned
with religious faith deriving from dependence on uncontrollable
natural forces, since the advance of science, he deems, is gradually
extinguishing this source.

For him, faith in a religion sanctioning a class society was essentially evidence of resignation in face of oppression. When resignation
began to turn into class consciousness and struggle against the
oppressors this could take the form not of rejection of all religion,
but of constructing a new one in which the values of the old one
were turned upside down. Engels argues that the urban proletariat
of the Roman Empire adopted the new religion of Christianity as a
religion of protest against slave-owners and their political allies, the
Emperor and his administration. In the Peasants' War we see the
German peasantry transforming the Lutheran protest against the
Papacy and its worldly corruption into a religiously sanctioned
attack on the feudal nobility who exploited them. Alienation is not
fully overcome when these religions of protest arise, for those who
join them still believe in a God-given order of society, not a man-
made one. But they insist that what their rulers called a God-given
order was in fact the work of the devil, or of evil men who had
twisted God's word to the world in order to gratify their desires
for wealth and power. They now assert their own right to interpret
God's word, and this is a big though not a total reassertion of human
power to re-create society. The Marxist would see a glimmering of
such reassertion even in those sects which have practised withdrawal
from society, or which have believed in purely supernatural means
of changing it, for instance in the imminent second coming of
Christ on the Day of Judgement. The interpretation of the Melanesian
cargo cults by Worsley is fundamentally Marxist, as we have seen
in the previous chapter. The religious expression of revolt is seen as
the precursor of a non-religious political movement. In respect of
capitalist society, some Marxist writers tend to interpret any kind
of Utopian religious movement in the working-class as a breaking
of the crust of traditional orthodoxy, and therefore a sign that class
consciousness is awakening. The failure of Utopian prophecies does

not matter; another attack on the problem will be made, and by a process of trial and error the correct analysis of their position will in the end be achieved.

It is interesting to note that the Marxist participants in the current effort at a Marxist-Catholic dialogue in France welcome and emphasise those elements in the Catholic position which stress human responsibility and creativity; they are not so interested in the Catholic social doctrine of the restraints on capitalist power which are necessary if there is to be a Christian social order.[17] A non-Marxist may well feel that Marx's contemporary followers have developed, beyond what the master would accept, the view that religious Utopianism represents the beginning of a rejection of alienation. Marx's own bitter criticism of Utopian Socialism assorts oddly with the tenderness shown towards religious sects by Bloch,[18] or towards left-wing Catholicism by some French Marxists.

Marx and Engels knew only one society with a well-developed proletariat, that of nineteenth-century England. They saw that this proletariat was largely uninterested in organised religion, whether sectarian or church-like. Engels wrote: 'Although English workers reject religion in practice without much conscious thought, they nevertheless recoil from an open admission of their lack of faith. Hard necessity will force the workers to give up their religious beliefs. They will come more and more to realise that these beliefs serve only to weaken the proletariat and to keep them obedient and faithful to the capitalist vampires'.[19] Many observers agreed with his assessment of the situation even though they interpreted it differently. Since his day, many other industrial countries have also experienced a decline in traditional Christian observance without any rise of new sectarian forms to take its place. This has happened both in Protestant countries, for example, Sweden, Norway, and Germany, and in Catholic ones such as France and Italy. According to the Marxist analysis this retreat from all religion should be a sign of the growth of a revolutionary class consciousness. But in fact its accompaniments on the political and industrial front have been very varied; in France and Italy a very substantial part of the working-class supports the Communist Party and Communist led trade unions, but in the Scandinavian countries and England the Labour Movement has developed strongly, but on very unrevolutionary lines. In both groups of countries the withdrawal from traditional religion extends far beyond the group of committed Socialists or Communists. Moreover some industrial countries, again both Protestant and Catholic, show a continuing high level of practice, and a much smaller differential between working- and middle-class level of practice. The USA, Holland and Belgium fall into this group.

These discrepancies with the predictions of the theory suggest that it is oversimplified; religious faith is not necessarily a sign of entire acceptance or rebellion against a social order. This complication is surely to be expected when we take account of the very varying relations between religious, political and economic organisation in different parts of the capitalist world. The Roman Catholic church, for instance, may appear in Spain as an established church with no tolerated rivals, in Italy and France as a church no longer privileged but historically associated with political and economic privilege, in Holland or England as the representative of a minority group which had to struggle for its rights against a Protestant majority, and in the USA as one denomination on an equal footing with a number of others. In one country it may traditionally have drawn its strength from the bourgeoisie, in another from the workers or the peasants. In all these different contexts it is unlikely to be seen always as simply the prop of the established social order. To point this out is to criticise the general Marxist view of a close relation between economic structure, political institutions and ideologies, both religious and political. It is my view that religions, except in isolated preliterate societies, do not stand in a close and regular relationship with social structures, in either their economic or political aspects.

The persistence of a substantially higher degree of religious practice in the USA than in Britain, or in Holland than in Sweden, puts a question-mark against another aspect of Marx's theory, the view that the practical power of science, and the spread of a scientific way of thinking, had, in the nineteenth century in Western Europe, removed the impetus to religious practice hitherto provided by fear of uncomprehended natural forces. This view is not specific to Marx, it was widely held by the positivist school of sociology, and reappears in the Freudian account. (There may be, of course, minor differences of opinion as to the date of the final triumph of science.) It is the unspoken premise of Engels' argument that whereas it was natural that the protest of slaves in the ancient world, or serfs in late medieval Germany, should have taken a religious form, it was equally natural that the protest of wage-slaves in nineteenth-century England should take a secular form. So far, so good, but it would seem to follow that all countries similar in their current use of scientific achievements should show the same level of religion and irreligion. As we have seen, this is not the case. A particular difficulty arises in the USA where traditional religious practice is not declining at all.

We can now sum up the Marxian view on the functions of religion. Religion is a necessary part of all class-divided societies, i.e., all those which have existed since primitive Communism came to an end. Its major function is to strengthen these class-ridden social structures; its minor one is to express and stimulate the first stirrings of criticism and discontent among the oppressed. But as all religions are false representations of reality, because they underestimate human powers of creation, religions can never be the vehicles of social revolutions. Religion has an identifiable function in society, but it is not a necessary and inevitable aspect of being human, as the functional school suggest. I think that Marx's basically optimistic view of human society is apparent here; man can pull himself up by his own bootstraps and cure himself of his religious addiction. Of course, there is nothing in this view to suggest that the new classless society may not develop some ritual celebrations of itself. But these would not be the beginnings of new religion because they would not represent submission to an unquestionable authority, but merely dramatise more vividly than everyday life the new creation of a just society, recognised as a human achievement and a human responsibility. Thus, while functional analysts of religion are tempted to see in Communist processions, pilgrimages and slogans a functional equivalent to religion, a necessary prop of the social order, Marxists will interpret them differently. A Communist society, by definition, has no need of a functional equivalent, for alienation is over.

It is noticeable how the Marxian and the Comtean view of ritual in the perfect future society differ. For Marx, since all participate in the new creation and are free to alter and re-create it, ritual can be no more than a celebration of this freedom, expressive, not instrumental. For Comte, since only the sociologist philosopher-kings can keep the new society on an even keel, ritual is an essential instrument by which to achieve and maintain consensus.

Marx's optimistic account of the future can be contrasted with the much more pessimistic account of human possibilities to be discovered in Freud's theory of religion. His ideas were first set out in *Totem and Taboo*,[20] were restated and elaborated in *Future of an Illusion*,[21] and were applied to the particular case of Judaism in *Moses and Monotheism*.[22] Some writers with strong Freudian sympathies have attempted to interpret Christianity along Freudian

lines, notably Pfister,[23] Lee[24] and Fromm.[25] As Pfister was, and
Lee is, a practising Christian minister, it is impossible to say that
Freud's ideas are necessarily destructive of religious faith. Though
he himself was a thoroughgoing atheist, he recognised that an
account of how people come to have a particular belief is not the
same as a proof or disproof of its truth.

Part of Freud's arguments rest on the now discredited anthropological generalisations put forward in Frazer's *Totemism and
Exogamy*, and part rest on a speculative reconstruction of the first
forms of human society, and on the notion of inherited racial
memory, now discredited by modern biology. If these parts made up
the whole, it would not be worthy of our consideration today. What
is worthy to be examined alongside other sociological theories of
religion is the set of ideas which arose from the clinical practice of
Freud and other analysts, the theory of how the infant develops into
an adult member of his society. Freud became convinced from his
clinical material, that every male child in growing up must develop
a strong ambivalence to his father, that is, he must feel both love
and hate, admiration and fear, believe him to be both protective
and destructive. (In a muted degree girls would develop a similar
ambivalence to their mothers, but Freud is little concerned with any
social effects of this 'Electra complex'.) He argues that from the
beginning the boy's love for his mother is possessive and strongly
tinged with sexuality, therefore he hates and fears his father as a
rival for his mother's affection. In fantasy he even injures and kills
his father in order to monopolise his mother's love and attention.
But these fantasies cause him acute guilt feelings because he also
feels love for his father as a protector and source of gratification.
Consequently his guilt expresses itself in the further fantasies of the
father wishing in revenge to kill and injure him, and of his being
able to appease this paternal hostility only by total submissive
obedience. Since the boy also begins to identify with the father and
take him for a model, this drama of guilt and its assuagement is now
played out within the boy's mind. The image of the father is intro-
jected and becomes the basis of the super-ego; it acts like the fantasy
father in punishing the aggressive and disobedient acts, or even
wishes, of the son with extreme severity.

At the same time as this Oedipal drama is developing, the boy is
also learning more and more about the real world. He learns early
to distinguish himself from his environment, to find a self distinct
from other persons with whom he interacts. This learning is largely
by frustration; he learns that wishes are not omnipotent, and fears

may be unrealistic. He learns that his parents are not omnipotent over him, and that neither their punishments or rewards are as he first imagined them. In particular he learns that his projections on to his father of an overwhelming desire to punish him for aggression and jealousy are unrealistic.

This learning, however, in Freud's view, is never complete, and does not touch Oedipal feelings and fantasies repressed into the unconscious mind. Freud firmly believed from his clinical evidence (remember that his first patients were hysterics) that fantasies of aggression, guilt and punishment, or of total and blissful love and union, were not within reach of gradual correction by subsequent experience of human relations in and outside the immediate family. They remained, and if, in particular situations of strain or invocation of old memories, they emerge from the unconscious and affect conscious activity, they colour this with their own powerful and ambivalent emotion towards father and father-figures. The only way to prevent unconscious fantasies from distorting realistic perception of the world and action on it, was by the technique of analysis, which controlled the release of unconscious material, and enabled the patient to see it as fantastic and unreal. In the absence of analysis, the neurotic at all times, and the normal person in times of stress, would have a picture of reality, particularly of real authority, distorted by Oedipal fantasies. The Oedipal fantasy of the father is, to Freud, the basis of belief in a god demanding worship and obedience and punishing sin.

The occasions of stress and fear which regularly provoke a regression to the infantile state of mind, and therefore a reactivation of the Oedipal feelings, are in Freud's view twofold. There is fear of natural forces, which men depend upon for survival but cannot control, and there is resentment at the continual frustrations of instinct which social living imposes on the individual. Such occasions of fear and frustration are not just incidents in individual life-histories, but affect many men at one time. Thus occurs a collective response to them, and individual fantasies and neurotic behaviour are merged into collective fantasy and religious ritual. While occasions of infantile behaviour arising out of the relations of men to nature may be reduced enormously by advances in wealth and technology, occasions arising out of society's frustration of the individual cannot be much diminished. Men have powerful instincts of love and aggression which must often be frustrated in the interests of social order. The first direction of love in the child's life is towards the mother, but this must be repressed by the incest taboo which is a basic rule of every society. The first object of aggression is the father, but this must be suppressed in the interests of family order, and because of the actual power of the father over the infant. Men are always to some extent at odds with their society, realising the benefits of cooperation but resenting the costs in instinctual frustration. In this basic view of humanity, Freud differs greatly from Marx. But in the way in which his theory is applied to religion certain similarities appear. Freud agrees with Marx that the lower orders have the greatest need for religion, because they suffer more from instinctual frustration than the ruling class. Religion for the masses serves to prevent their rebellion, their demand for at least an equal chance of gratifying their desires. While the ruling class enjoy not only a higher level of actual satisfaction, but also vicarious satisfaction through art and literature, the masses, lacking both, require compensatory fantasies in their religions. Also Freud agrees with Marx that a less religious society is one in which more social experiment is possible. Freud argues that through the fantasies of the punishing super-ego, religiously sanctioned ethics have always imposed more restrictions on human instincts than are justified as necessary to a peaceful and orderly society. Imposing these more severe restrictions increases the occasions of frustration, and the occasions for arousing infantile guilt-feelings. These once aroused can only be satisfied by further restrictions and thus a vicious circle may be set up; but this circle may be broken, and a more beneficent one come into being, through the advance of science. Science gives control and security against threats of natural disaster, and thus reduces the occasions of panic and anxiety which evoke the Oedipal feelings. Religious belief then becomes less intense, and the exploration of the grounds and consequences of particular moral codes becomes permissible. Experience can be brought to bear, and a more utilitarian approach to morality gains ground.

Thus, as with Marx, Freud argues that, provided there is a powerful growth of natural science, human creativity can have some scope in determining social structure, provided it is not inhibited by religious belief. But the sort of creativity shown by religious sects which demand a totally new beginning, and look forward to a Utopia in this world or the next, are more suspect to Freudian than to Marxist thought. To a Freudian these betray very clearly their unconscious origins, and therefore their unrealistic hopes. Realistic reconstruction of society must always be aware of the limits of possible harmony in a society, and of rationality among its members. Because of these limits it is likely that though religions may change in form and content, they will always persist. Men have a continuing need of their religion because it both expresses their neurosis and channels it so that it does not appear as an abnormality interfering with their daily lives. Thus, to Freud, the various types of mass political and social enthusiasm would be classed as religions, or functional equivalents to religion. The cause of religion lies in the particular difficulties of the socialisation process in the human family, and the inevitable conflicts of individual and collective interest in human society. The function of it is to support a given social order, though on occasion there can be religious expressions of rebellion against it.

Critics of Freud have claimed that whatever its merits, his theory has no place in the sociology of religion since it is psychological in character. At the best all it can explain are some general character-istics of all religion, and not the variety amongst them that the sociologist wants to make intelligible. For instance, granting that all gods are in some sense parent-figures, why is the balance between male and female deities so different in different systems? Why are some gods personal and transcendent, while others are more impersonal and immanent? Why is sacrifice, even human sacrifice, so important in some religions, yet non-existent in others? This criticism has weight, but it still remains possible that a sociological explanation of these variations will be unconvincing unless some-thing like the Freudian ground-base of human nature is brought in as one element in the whole. I would also submit that Freudian theory does put forward some testable propositions, for example, the interconnectedness of the advance of natural science, moral permissiveness, utilitarianism in ethics, and loss of religious intensity. It might also be tested in respect of sects, by assessing how far they all display the characteristics of a new quasi-familial community, with the new leader as the perfectly good parent of infantile fantasy and adult longing, and the old religion and society as utterly hostile and evil. I think Freud's ideas here may provide a useful supplement to the thesis that sects arise among those who suffer relative social deprivation.

The original weakness of Freud's theory was not its generality but the way in which findings about a limited number of personalities in one society were generalised into statements about all human personality development. This weakness has now to some extent been remedied, for Freud's thesis about the particular difficulties of socialisation of the child now have some backing from biological and ethological studies of primate, including human, behaviour.

These studies cannot corroborate the Freudian view of the 'unconscious' as a compartment of the mind, but they do strongly indicate the basic importance of conjugal and parental roles in human society, the lasting influence of infantile experience on subsequent social relationships, and the ambivalence between love and aggression in intra-familial relations.

1. J. M. Yinger, *Religion, Society and the Individual*, 1957.
   —*Sociology Looks at Religion*, 1963.
2. T. F. O'Dea, *The Sociology of Religion*, 1966.
3. P. Berger, *The Social Reality of Religion*, 1969.
4. T. Luckmann, *The Invisible Religion*, 1967.
5. J. M. Yinger, op. cit., p. 9.
6. J. M. Yinger, op. cit., p. 69.
7. P. Berger, *The Social Reality of Religion*, p. 87.
8. W. Herberg, *Protestant, Catholic, Jew*, 1960, revised ed.
9. B. Wilson, *Religion in Secular Society*, 1966.
10. T. Luckmann, op. cit., p. 49.
11. T. F. O'Dea, op. cit., p. 31.
12. T. F. O'Dea, op. cit., p. 27.
13. Marx's views are expounded most systematically in *The Theses on Feuerbach*. See also the Marx–Engels *Anthology on Religion*, 1958.
14. F. Engels, 'On the History of Early Christianity', *Die Neue Zeit*, vol. I, 1894.
15. F. Engels, *The Peasant War in Germany*, English trans., 1927.
16. F. Engels, *State of the Working Class in England in 1844*, 1958, English ed., p. 270.
17. R. Garaudy, *From Anathema to Dialogue—the Challenge of Marxist–Christian Cooperation*, 1967.
18. E. Bloch, 'Utopie et Marxisme', *Archives de Sociologie des Réligions*, 1966.
19. F. Engels, *State of the Working Class in England in 1844*, p. 270.
20. S. Freud, *Totem and Taboo*, 1913.
21. S. Freud, *Future of an Illusion*, 1962, revised ed.
22. S. Freud, *Moses and Monotheism*, 1939.
23. O. Pfister, *Christianity and Fear*, 1948.
24. R. S. Lee, *Freud and Christianity*, 1948.
25. E. Fromm, *Psychoanalysis and Religion*, 1950.
   —*The Dogma of Christ*, 1963.

5

CHURCH, SECT AND DENOMINATION

The publication by Ernst Troeltsch in 1919 of *The Social Teachings of the Christian Churches* effectively launched the sociological study of religion in Christian societies. Though his analysis deliberately stopped short of the modern industrial period, his leading ideas have been made use of by others in the study of this later period also.

Troeltsch's starting-point is the development, immediately after the death of Jesus, of the doctrine of Christ as the redeemer who had left to his church the means of grace and salvation through the sacraments, and as the teacher who had proclaimed a law of love for all mankind. The new communities, in order to work together, needed to define the position of Christ in such a way as to mark it off clearly from the polytheistic gods of the contemporaneous mystery cults, and to link it with the monotheistic God of the Jewish prophets. There resulted a trinitarian doctrine which has always been open to three rather different interpretations, and therefore has led to the 'three main types of the sociological development of Christian thought; the church, the sect and mysticism'.[1] The relative importance of these three types, and the interrelations between them, will be affected by various social factors, but all derive from the essential gospel teaching, and therefore all will coexist in tension with one another, so long as Christianity endures. Troeltsch's definitions of church, sect and mystic group I will give in his own words:[2] 'The church is an institution which has been endowed with grace and salvation as the result of the work of Redemption; it is able to receive the masses and adjust itself to the world, because to a certain extent it can afford to ignore the need for subjective holiness for the sake of the objective treasures of grace and redemption. The sect is a voluntary society composed of strict and definite Christian believers bound to each other by the fact that all have experienced "the new birth". These believers live apart from the world, are limited to small groups, emphasise the law instead of grace, and in varying degrees within their own circle set up the Christian order based on love; all this is done in preparation for and expectation of the coming Kingdom of God. Mysticism means that the world of ideas which had hardened into formal worship and doctrine is transformed into a purely personal and inward experience; this leads to the formation of groups on a purely personal basis, with no permanent form, which also tend to weaken the significance of forms of worship, doctrine and the historical element.'

The church-type of Christianity is the only one which can include all sorts and conditions of men. It necessarily lays stress on the sacraments, the priesthood and the organisation of teaching and practice to secure religious uniformity. To include all people, to appeal to all people, it has to compromise with rigorous ethical demands, and accept that because of man's sin, and to remedy its consequences as far as may be, institutions of government and property are necessary. It expects neither a necessary though gradual progress to moral perfection on this earth, nor an imminent second coming of Christ. The city of God will always be different from the city of men. In order to preserve what it deems to be objective religious truths, it is ready to cooperate with and receive help from the state and other social institutions. In Christian history, the church-type is represented by the Catholic, the Eastern Orthodox, the Lutheran and the Calvinist confessions.

The sect, according to Troeltsch, 'belongs essentially to the lower classes, and therefore does not need to come to terms with thought in general. It has no theology, and possesses only a strict ethic, a living Mythos, and a passionate hope for the future'.[3] Troeltsch is not arguing that sectarian Christianity simply reflects a lower-class resentment or aspiration, only that true sectaries are drawn from the ranks of those classes, since it is from their viewpoint that compromise with the world, the flesh and the devil looks most immoral and least necessary. Mysticism, on the other hand, may arise as a 'refuge for the religious life of the cultured classes',[4] or in other social milieux. The value placed by the mystic on personal inward experience usually includes a depreciation of sensual pleasures, of striving for power, wealth or knowledge. Therefore mystic groups tend to agree with sects in the practice of a more ascetic kind of life, but they see this as the best preparation for achieving mystical union with Christ rather than as an end in itself. They do not organise to confound or condemn the church, but accept in effect only that part of her doctrines and practice which help them to their supremely important personal experiences. Whilst the leader can be an example and guide to his followers, yet each must, in the end, find his own way to the mystical experience; the discipline exerted by leaders over followers, or by the group over its members, is less than in the sect, where all are encouraged to strenuous moral effort, and perhaps proselytising activity as well. Troeltsch conceives both mystic and sectarian groups not only as a necessary, but as a useful, supplement to the church. The compromise that the church makes with the world must be remade again and again as social conditions change; sectaries and mystics help in this continual adjustment of the rigorous morality of the gospels to what Troeltsch calls an 'ethic of civilisation'.[5] This process of adjustment Troeltsch traces in his history; in the first period of Christian history, the Catholic Church establishes itself as the means of salvation to all men. It moderates the demands of the gospel ethic in order to become and remain comprehensive, but allows religious orders to develop as a means whereby those called to a fuller realisation of the gospel teaching may follow their vocation. This development of the church, from the second century A.D. onwards, was not without sectarian challenge. Even before the close connection with Roman imperial power was established in the fourth century, marking a further stage in the process of compromise with the world, there were groups such as the Marcionites, Montanists and Donatists who proclaimed a return to a more ascetic way of life, and set up organisations cut off from the Catholic Church. Sectarian outbreaks revived during the Middle Ages, varying from ephemeral millenarian movements such as the Pastoureaux in France in the thirteenth and fourteenth centuries, to well-organised and enduring movements such as the Cathari in Bulgaria, southern France and Italy. Some were heretical and antagonistic to the church at every point, as were the Cathari; some were of a kind that in slightly different circumstances might have been recognised as an order rather than repudiated as a sect. Such was the movement led by Peter Waldo, the Poor Men of Lyons, in twelfth-century France, which was closely similar to, and contemporary with, the movement of St Francis of Assisi. Yet St Francis and his followers were eventually accepted into the bosom of the church; the followers of Peter Waldo began a career of centuries of persecution.

The significance of the Protestant Reformation lay in the abandonment of a dual standard of morality for clergy and laity. To the reformers, all men had a God-given calling whose obligations should be fully met. All were called, in their various capacities, to be 'monks in the world'. The Lutheran reformers did not go far in revising the traditional Christian morality of politics and economic life, but they emphasised the spontaneous love which would flow from a true and lively faith in Christ, and which would redeem personal morality. That sin would still corrupt states and rulers, and yet make them necessary, was taken almost for granted. Although Lutheranism became church-like in its comprehensiveness, in its readiness to accept saints and sinners alike, its particular form of compromise with the world bears one of the marks of medieval sectarianism, passivity and withdrawal from an inevitably wicked world. Yet, accepting the protection of rulers, it was not fully withdrawn from the world of politics. In economic matters, it saw no hope that a market economy could be moralised, and therefore clung to traditional practices which inhibited economic development.

Calvinist Protestantism also substituted the doctrine of the calling for the dual morality of Catholicism, but interpreted it as requiring the building of a new holy community. This new Zion would be fully in the world of sinful men, yet always struggling towards Christian perfection, as Calvinists saw it outlined in holy scripture. Their ethic drew rather more from Old Testament law than did the ideal ethic of Catholicism, yet many elements were common. But in their struggle to realise their ideal of a comprehensive and disciplined church in all of Western Europe, Calvinists used the weapons of war and wealth, and took the power of the state as their tool and ally. Thus they were forced into the same state of compromise with the gospel ethic of brotherly love as the Catholic Church itself.

Under pressure from the external threat of Protestantism, and from mounting criticism within, Catholicism itself underwent a form of reformation in the sixteenth and seventeenth centuries. Many new religious orders whose members worked in the world were begun, and some attempts made to release the papacy from its entanglements with wealth and political alliances. Mystic groups also played a part in the achievements of the Counter-Reformation. The interplay of these forces resulted in a new adjustment of Christian beliefs to the new social conditions of emergent Nationalism and capitalism. There arose the four 'compromising' churches of Lutheranism, Calvinism, Anglicanism and Catholicism. But alongside them still arose sects dissatisfied with any of these 'ethics of civilisation'. Some, in trying to realise fully the ideal of the Sermon on the Mount, suffered persecution passively, and avoided martyrdom only if they could find a home beyond the effective arm of prince or church. Others were militant, and tended to rely for inspiration on the Apocalypse of St John as well as the gospels. The groups of Anabaptists (believers in adult baptism) who eventually became known as the Moravians and Mennonites are typical of the first kind of sect, the Munster experiment under John of Leyden, or the fifth-monarchy men in Cromwell's armies, represent the second. Many of these sects had but a short life, and died out as the four churches developed a *modus vivendi* among themselves and in their relations with states, in the seventeenth and eighteenth centuries. Or the sectarian impulses stopped short of an act of secession (or expulsion by the church) as in Lutheran and Calvinist Pietism, the evangelical revival within Anglicanism, and the Wesleyan movement during the lifetime of its founder.

Although Troeltsch did not continue the history of church, sect and mysticism into the period of industrialisation in Europe, he did venture some comments on it. He believed that the advance of literacy and science on the one hand, and the particular social problems thrown up by industrial society on the other, both threaten the church-type of Christianity. He saw the response of the Catholic Church as a highly defensive effort to insist on old values, and on its right to a position of privilege because it was the repository of essential religious truths. Its critique of industrial society was ineffective because presented in terms of a paternalist alternative which seemed to look backwards instead of forwards. The Protestant churches, on the other hand, had responded to the new developments by adjusting their creeds and limiting their claim on their members and on the state. They had thus laid themselves widely open to sectarian and mystical influences. So far as they responded at all to the moral challenge of industrial society, it was to endorse the liberal utilitarian view which saw the values of freedom and abundance as a permanent gain, and the evils of class conflict and inequality as a temporary cost. Troeltsch thought that neither the Protestant nor the Catholic position represented an 'ethic of civilisation' appropriate to the contemporary social problem, whilst the directly sectarian alternatives appealed only to a few. He also recognised that the old tensions between church, sect and mysticism now operated in a much more complex situation, since there were also powerful non-religious schools of thought. Challenge to the church could now come from science, and from secular reformist and revolutionary movements, and these could also challenge the sects and mystic groups. Thus, though he firmly believed that there are 'permanent ethical values contained within the varied history of Christian social doctrines',[6] he concluded that whatever new solutions to social problems are conceived, they will emerge from contemporary systems of thought, not just from the New Testament, and will bear the inevitable marks of compromise with resistant facts, and transient appropriateness to an ever-changing situation.

One aspect of the comprehensive and compromising church which Troeltsch particularly examines is its relations with the state. He divides the history of these relations up to the Reformation into four periods. In the first three centuries of the Christian era, Christian communities only gradually grew to church-like status; their relation to the state was one of aloofness and indifference, except when persecution forced them into active hostility. There was a big development of philosophy within the growing church, but little exploration within it of political problems. On the other hand, the attempt to link the different congregations into a single hierarchical organisation threw up political problems within the church itself, which contributed to early sectarian manifestations.

Troeltsch's second period is that of the 'imperial church', from A.D. 300–500, when a parallel development of the civil and ecclesiastical expression of Roman imperial power occurred. The parallelism was never perfect, if only because the church acknowledged the Bishop of Rome as its head, whilst the secular administration looked to an emperor whose seat was at Constantinople. Yet emperors sought Christian unity as a buttress of their power, and bishops welcomed privileges granted by the Emperor as aids to the extension of the faith and the control of scattered communities. Troeltsch limits his further analysis to the developments in Western Christendom, and so suggests the sixth century as roughly the end of the 'imperial church'. But I think this category was applicable for very much longer in Eastern Christendom. The 'imperial church' collapsed in the West when the Emperor's writ ceased to run in his Western provinces, but continued under the Byzantine emperors in the East, until its last vestiges were swept away when the Turks captured Constantinople in 1453.

Troeltsch's next period in the West is that of the 'territorial church', and extends from the seventh to the twelfth centuries. It was marked by the disintegration of imperial authority into feudal fragments based on military power and land tenure. The central authority of the church underwent a similar process of fragmentation, with the growth of ecclesiastical landed property, and the treatment of ecclesiastical offices as the private property of the leading families of each district.

This tendency was reversed in the twelfth century by a series of reforming popes who by a strenuous conflict with feudal magnates and an equally strenuous effort to insist on clerical celibacy, tried to separate the civil and ecclesiastical administration. So far as they succeeded, they increased enormously the power of the papacy, and created a 'universal church'. The papacy claimed, and to a large extent exercised, the right to organise the church regardless of other political units, be they cities, feudal principalities, or nascent monarchies. No doubt this effective rebuilding of a centralised ecclesiastical administration was helped by the same forces which aided the construction of larger states, namely the revival of commerce, town life and the circulation of money. In reviving its separate administration, the church also revived its right to determine the sphere of 'things pertaining to salvation', and to criticise the exercise of power by secular authorities whose rights, in theory, ceased if they overstepped the bounds of Christian morality as interpreted by the pope and his bishops. The ideal was to use the separateness of the church as a point of vantage from which to penetrate and purify the world. Thus there would come into existence a Christian society in which, under the guidance of the Christian ethic, the different roles of ruler, soldier, priest, peasant and craftsman would be harmoniously related in an organic unity. Though all human institutions were marred by sin, the reforming power of the church in society was stressed. But the very process of removing the church from feudal entanglements depended on conditions which led the church into new forms of compromise with the world. The papacy was a political power, like the secular states, and was therefore involved in European diplomacy. Its power, though great, was never effectively beyond challenge by states singly or in alliance, and therefore it practised the arts of politics and war to rebut the challenge. Being so powerful, it attracted the power-seekers, who corrupted its Christian purposes still further. Finally the growth of town life and trade created new groups in which the sectarian impulse to a more rigorous ethic of equality and charity showed itself. Thus the medieval church is marked by the growth of new orders, and by sectarian heresy and mystical teachers. The recurrent 'weavers' heresies' are typical. The greater the claims by the spokesmen for orthodoxy that a powerful united church could penetrate and purify the world, the larger the perceived gap between promise and fulfilment, and the more frequent the sectarian or mystical criticism. The vantage point, if it ever existed outside the minds of scholars and idealists, was lost, as the papacy had to contend with powerful states who had copied the administrative example of the church in building up centralised power.

The Reformation can therefore be seen as a culmination of trends in church-sect and church-state relations, as well as a new beginning. In both Catholic and Protestant countries, it tended to end in an Erastian situation, i.e., the kings and princes supervised ecclesiastical organisation in their own countries. Medieval popes had already recognised the *ecclesia anglicana* as an administrative entity within the Catholic Church. The Tudor religious settlement which established the Church of England used this separate identity as a means of repudiating papal supremacy. The architects of a settlement did not reject the idea of a universal church; they rejected the view that a consequence of its universality was the acceptance of papal claims. The Spanish and French monarchies made effective inroads against papal authority, even though they did not deny it altogether, and from time to time appeared as its champions. The Austrian Hapsburgs, having used the papalist Society of Jesus to re-establish Catholicism as the sole religion of their territories, later fought against and reduced the power of the pope in their empire. The Lutheran churches from the beginning were organised as state-churches, of Saxony, Prussia, Sweden, etc. The Calvinists tried to establish something like a universal and dominant church, not dissimilar in its relations with states to the medieval papal supremacy of the High Middle Ages, but they found the conditions for its establishment unpropitious. Calvinism then either fell back into a sectarian position, as with the Huguenots in seventeenth-century France, and the Baptists and Independents in England, or found a power base in a secular state, as Calvin himself dominated the canton of Geneva, or helped to set up the United Provinces as a separate state in the Netherlands. Only where they were able to begin completely new communities across the Atlantic in New England could they develop an organisation in which religious institutions for a time dominated secular ones.

Troeltsch argued that church-state relations threw light on the kind and degree of compromise with the ethical ideal of Christianity which a church had arrived at, and therefore on the kind of sectarian or mystical activity which the compromise provoked. This point has been taken up by Werner Stark who attempts to explain all sectarianism in terms of church-state relations.[7] He draws a distinction between 'established churches', those which accept privileges accorded them by particular states, and whose boundaries are effectively coterminous with the state, and 'universal churches', which have an organisation distinct from the state, and claim members beyond the bounds of any one state. He argues that in the former case the close link of church and state pushes the inevitable compromise with worldly values much farther than in the latter case, and therefore provokes more resentment and dissatisfaction among the unprivileged and the ethical rigorists. This greater resentment and discontent gives rise to sects. He concedes that a universal church also has to make some compromise of Christian ethical values, but the criticism that this evokes can be channelled into new groups, such as the religious orders, which, as they remain inside the church, can the more effectively attack complacency and worldliness. In his view the only true universal church of Christendom since the Reformation has been the Roman Catholic Church, since the Calvinist attempt at that status failed. All others are 'established churches', and the Anglican and Russian Orthodox churches have been the most extreme members of that class.

He then goes on to show that since the Reformation, sectarianism has been at a minimum in Roman Catholic countries, and at a maximum in Russia and England. He also tries to show that Catholicism has been more critical of political and social injustice, particularly that it has been much more critical of industrial capitalist society, than the established Protestant churches.

Stark's radical distinction between established and universal churches is, I think, misleading. Since the Reformation, and in most cases before, all European states have achieved some degree of control of religious organisation within their boundaries, and this has limited the independence of both Catholic and Protestant churches. But the Catholic Church has not only suffered state intervention, it has also frequently enjoyed state privilege, indeed the typical concordat of state and church spelt out both aspects in detail. In terms of privilege, it would be hard to argue that the Catholic Church in pre-revolutionary France, or in Spain and Portugal today, was less 'established' than, say, eighteenth-century or contemporary Anglicanism. Equally, it would be hard to prove that the church-state link in Anglicanism of the sixteenth and seventeenth centuries was closer than the equivalent link in the Lutheran churches of the period. Yet clearly the incidence of sectarianism was greater in England than in either Lutheran countries or the Catholic countries of France, Spain and Portugal. In Lutheranism the one substantial movement of ethical idealism and mysticism was Pietism, but this never moved right out of the church, but remained as a group of societies within it. In the 'established' Catholic Church of France there occurred Jansenism and Quietism, which in different ways criticised the church, but both died out after a short struggle. In Spain and Italy sectarianism has been minimal, despite strong 'establishment' of Catholicism.

Given that the Anglican Church is definitely 'established' rather than universal, it is still difficult to accept the correlation of this fact with the rise and fall of sects. I would argue that the strongest degree of establishment existed in the late seventeenth and in the eighteenth centuries, when civil disabilities were imposed on all non-Anglicans, and the political entanglement and worldliness of the Anglican Church was a by-word. Yet in that period all the old sects declined, very few new ones cropped up, and the big movement of revival and criticism, whether Wesleyan or Evangelical, which grew up at the end of the eighteenth century was from within the church. The real challenge to Anglicanism from outside occurred during the nineteenth century, a time when the extent of Anglican privilege was being reduced, not extended.

It seems that the only case where a change in church-state relations towards greater establishment was associated with sectarianism was that of Russia. The church in Russia up to the mid-seventeenth century was an established church, but in a rather decayed condition. A great deal of the power of patronage had fallen into the hands of landlords or peasant communities, who could choose their own priest for their own church. Peter the Great and his predecessor strove to achieve a more centralised and more subservient church, and provoked the schism of the 'Old Believers'. Though the origins of the later sects are obscure, it may be that they also expressed a resentment of the Muscovite bureaucracy and of Greater Russian dominance over the other nationalities in the empire.

Clearly a proper test of Stark's thesis of the causal association of 'established' churches with sectarianism requires investigation of all occurrences of each of these phenomena before the attempt at correlation is made. What he gives us is an examination of two instances apparently favourable to his thesis, tsarist Russia and Anglican England, and an attempt to explain an apparently contrary instance, i.e., sectarian religion in the USA, as in fact conforming to his thesis. The interest of the American scene to him is that it has always shown a great number and variety of sects, yet no one confession is 'by law established'; in fact, the constitution forbids any 'established church'. Why have the sects nevertheless proliferated?

His answer starts from the observation that American society, since independence, has shown strong cleavages between the settled east and the changing frontier west, between the creditor and merchant in the east and the farmer-debtor in the west, and latterly between the workers and the capitalists in industry. The Protestant denominations in the old settled areas were inevitably associated with the resented power and privilege of these regions; therefore in the frontier regions they were unable to establish themselves, and sects took their place. In the case of Episcopalians (equivalent to Anglicans in England) and of the Congregationalists (growing from the Independents who first settled in New England) there was a failure to keep members in the new areas. In the case of Methodists and Baptists there was a schism in the group, congregations from the frontier areas splitting off from the parent body. And the process of secession and innovation was repeated several times in both these denominations. Apart from the conflicts of economic interest between the east and the new regions, there was a contrast in styles of life which made different religious styles appropriate. The new settlers demanded a more emotional and spontaneous religion, and were less deferential to theological scholarship and a professional ministry. 'Hell-fire preaching' and camp-meeting revivalism met their religious needs better. These factors of economic and cultural conflict explain, in Stark's view, the origin of sectarianism in America. These reappeared, in slightly different form, when the great new industrial towns were growing up in the mid-nineteenth century and onwards. But sectarianism was limited there because Protestants of the old stock did not populate these towns as they had predominantly populated the frontier during the great expansion. The mass of new immigrants to the towns came directly from Europe, bringing their Catholic, Lutheran or Jewish faiths with them. Their religions, being already different from the 'unofficial establishments' of Protestant denominations, could be adapted to sectarian purposes, and used as a vehicle of ethnic identity, of protest against social injustice, and of defence against anomie. Thus, despite their traditional 'church' status, Catholicism, Judaism and Lutheranism performed for the mass of new urban immigrants the same functions as the Protestant sects performed for the immigrants into the new frontier areas. Finally, Stark argues that sectarianism is a much diminished force in modern America. Society is so much more homogeneously American that there is no longer an 'unofficial establishment' of Protestantism, confronted by a large number of sects, or ethnic churches serving the same function. Rather there is a multiplicity of denominations who can live comfortably together because the effective creed of all of them is the 'American way of life'. Sectarianism is limited to the few disprivileged groups still remaining, particularly the Negroes, and to those groups already disenchanted with the moral and materialistic optimism of the 'American way of life'. Apart from these, there is only the surface diversity to be expected in a society where complete religious toleration is coupled with near unanimity in basic values.

This analysis of American religion derives largely from the work of H. R. Niebuhr[8] and Will Herberg.[9] Illuminating though it is, it does not succeed in fitting American experience into Stark's generalisation about sects and established churches. If membership in legally unestablished religious groups, such as the Congregationalists or Presbyterians in America, can be repudiated on account of their social conservatism, it is surely possible that membership in a universal church which happens to be wealthy and socially conservative may also be rejected. Stark notes, correctly, that Catholic countries in recent centuries have not experienced sectarianism to the same degree as some Protestant ones; he does not mention, but must be aware of, the powerful secular movements of protest against the church, or outside the church, in some Catholic countries. He argues that a Catholic critique of capitalism has always existed, modifying the seeming acceptance of wealth and power by the church, but that established Protestant churches have been silent, or have even become apologists for capitalism. Yet in some industrialised countries the working class has largely deserted the church, whether Protestant or Catholic. In France and Italy proletarian religious practice is as limited as in England. It seems that Stark overestimates the effectiveness of Christian programmes of social reform, and that Troeltsch was nearer the mark when he argued that neither Catholic nor Protestant had yet found an 'ethic of civilisation' which would re-establish them as comprehensive churches in fact, as well as in history and in hope.

The main value of Stark's work is in showing in detail how Calvinism aimed at church-like status and how it failed, and in bringing the history of Russian sects fully into the picture. Too often sectarianism is discussed as if it were purely a West European and American phenomenon.

Stark tried to understand sects better by looking at the differences between churches. Other writers who have taken up Troeltsch's hypotheses have tried to understand them better by looking more closely at their internal structure and social context. I will try to summarise briefly the work in this field of H. R. Niebuhr, Bryan Wilson[10] and D. A. Martin.[11]

Niebuhr's study of religion in the USA led him to believe that a pure sect-type religion is always transient. A sect either dies or changes into a denomination, a group which is less at odds with society at large, and which tolerates and is tolerated by other religious groups. He accepts the view that sects are born as a protest against worldliness which the churches have condoned. At the beginning, the members of a sect are all volunteers, and as they may have joined it at some cost, they tend to have a total commitment to it. The strength of their loyalty is often manifest in personal devotion to a charismatic leader who has gathered the new group around him. Sect membership for the original volunteers is the most important status they have, and enthusiasm runs high. As time goes on, however, the nature of commitment to the sect necessarily alters, and the level of enthusiasm is lowered. Members by birth become a larger proportion of the total, and are likely to be less completely committed than the volunteers. The original leader dies, and his successor may not be able to evoke the same personal loyalty (if he does do so among part of the following, there is likely to be a further split in the sect). The second great change over time results from the upward social mobility which sect membership engenders. Sect morality, as a counterblast to worldly indulgence, preaches hard work, thrift, and sexual discipline to the individual, charity and warm brotherliness to the group. Sect members may be originally recruited from the poorest, but as they follow these precepts they get richer, and as they get richer and more secure they will be less hostile to the world. If their sect remains socially radical they will leave it, but if enough members experience this upward social movement together, the whole group will move into a more tolerant posture *vis-à-vis* the world and other groups. The movement away from sectarianism may not be only along a line from radicalism to conservatism; it may be manifest in a more favourable attitude to an educated ministry, in a more sober and unemotional form of worship, in a movement away from biblical fundamentalism and millennial hopes. In any or all of these ways, a sect which lasts beyond the first generation moves towards a denominational position, and begins to resemble the groups that it began by rejecting. Since there was no pressure of persecution to intensify enthusiasm, and since opportunities for upward social movement were abundant, this process of denominationalisation has been particularly speedy in the USA. Niebuhr documents several examples, particularly the adaptation of frontier-type Methodism and Baptism to the more settled and affluent conditions of nineteenth- and twentieth-century America, and the changes within the sect of the Disciples of Christ, born in 1844, towards the middle-class ethos and the acceptance of the status of one Protestant denomination amongst others.

His work, however, has not gone unchallenged; it stands as a summation of positive instances rather than as a general theory of the natural history of sects. Wilson has argued against it that only some sects are susceptible to the denominationalising process; this has led him to a further classification of sects and a closer analysis of the mutual influence of sect and surrounding society. Martin has argued against it that a religious group can be a denomination from the beginning; it does not have to be the transformation of an earlier sect.

Within the broad group of sects Wilson distinguishes four types: conversionist, adventist, introversionist and gnostic. The first puts the highest value on rapid evangelism; the second believes in the imminence of the end of the world, the second coming of Christ, or some other impending divine intervention; the third puts the highest value on maintaining purity of doctrine and working out its version of Christian ethics within the group; the fourth proclaims, not new values, but a technique for achieving existing religious and worldly values. Sects vary according to the conditions of their emergence; Wilson describes them as generally due to 'stresses and tensions differentially experienced within the total society'.[12] He thinks that the strains of sudden urbanisation and industrialisation tend to engender a conversionist type of sect, whereas the adventist and introversionist types recruit their followers from among those suffering 'longer persisting deprivations'.

The type of sect and the circumstances of its origin affect its internal structure. The introversionist sect will try to isolate itself physically, or insulate itself socially, from all non-members. Contacts outside the bounds of the sect are to be limited as far as possible. The community or congregation tends to be the most important social unit, although some degree of organisation linking these units may exist, or be gradually developed. Since sect membership entails so much, members are not lightly accepted, and informal group discipline is likely to be very effective. On the other hand, the conversionist sect will organise for widespread proselytisation, and to that end will administer its resources centrally, and develop a professional ministry. Members are easily accepted; in favourable times membership swells rapidly, and control and discipline of members is less effective. The distinctive message of the sect may get blurred and imprecise.

Both the aims and the internal organisation of the sect are affected by external factors. Most important among these are the degree of religious toleration, and of religious pluralism, and factors promoting or inhibiting sectarian recruitment in each case. Toleration, of course, is a matter of fact as well as law. The establishment of freedom of religion in the American constitution did not prevent a great deal of suspicion and intolerance of the first Mormon community. This intolerance provoked the trek beyond the frontier and the final settlement in the territory of Utah, and was thus a factor in the physical separateness of the Mormons, and their consequent ability to build a new kind of religious community. Once this physical separateness was achieved, there could be, and was, very widespread and successful missionary enterprise without the danger of diluting sectarian values.

The early history of the Quakers shows that the success or otherwise of missionary enterprise may alter the type of sect, and consequently affect its internal structure also. The Quakers began as a socially radical conversionist sect depending on charismatic leaders like George Fox and James Nayler. But after great initial successes, their numbers declined, and the group became much more introversionist in character. It was marked off plainly from the outside world by speech, dress and way of living, and by the growth of a rule of endogamy. Its social radicalism remained, but was concentrated on a few issues, notably war and slavery, and its organisation became very egalitarian, relying on a belief in the achievement of unanimity rather than on the majority vote.

Wilson concludes that conversionist sects are more likely to arise in a setting of tolerance and democratic pluralism, and that their particular ideology and internal structure puts them at the greatest risk of moving towards denominational status. Conversionist sects have also been at risk because they have worked largely among urbanising and industrialising populations, and thus 'accommodated people whose social marginality and sense of anomie were often temporary, a consequence of inadequate adjustment to rapidly changing social conditions'.[13] It is of course true that adventist sects such as Jehovah's Witnesses may attempt large-scale conversion, but their message is so much at odds with established opinion and knowledge, not only with religious beliefs, that their enterprise is not likely to be very successful, whereas a conversionist sect which preaches a simple gospel of sin and repentance and the saving power of Christ may have much greater numerical success. Adventist sects in recent times therefore have had less risk of becoming denominations.

The position of the gnostic sect differs from all three of the others. It differs from established values and beliefs in only a few points, and these are matters of means rather than ends. Wilson's example is Christian Science and its attitude to orthodox medicine; another example would be Scientology and its hostility to psychiatry. As the gnostic sect shares many values, e.g., those of health, prosperity and adjustment to the world, with the rest of society, it is already somewhat denominational. But the points which it does not share, the special knowledge or gnosis which it claims, are so radically inconsistent with accepted opinion that widespread conversion to the gnostic sect is most unlikely. Therefore the dilution of doctrine which large numbers of adherents might produce is avoided. Studies of recruitment to Christian Science suggest that only those who have had personal experience of successful faith-healing are likely to be converted. Mrs Eddy, the founder of the sect, had this experience very dramatically herself.

Wilson's mode of analysis shows that conditions in the USA in the nineteenth century were particularly propitious to the emergence of conversionist sects which would turn into denominations. But even in America he finds instances of what he calls 'established sects', that is, sects which have maintained themselves as such for several generations.

Examples of established sects in Britain are the Christadelphians and the Salvation Army, both over a century old, and the various branches of the Brethren which all stem from an evangelical movement in Dublin in 1827. An interesting feature of the last case is the clear intensification of doctrinal and social segregation of the members; sectarian characteristics have in fact grown stronger with age. Wilson tackles the problem of upward social mobility in established sects, and shows that this can occur without the consequence of denominationalisation. He also shows that there are sects, such as the Brethren, which did not begin amongst the poorest or most disorganised sections of the population. In an established sect there is usually some tendency to occupational specialisation, because some jobs are thought to be morally wrong in themselves, or likely to necessitate particular wrong actions. But this occupational specialisation does not preclude upward mobility, and might even facilitate it, since being an independent business man or worker is generally thought to be the morally safest position. No doubt some upwardly mobile members leave their sect, but an upward move in the average social level of the membership is possible without a lessening of social exclusiveness. Perhaps it is significant that sectarian social ethics tend to criticise the corruption of the state rather than the immorality of wealth.

Wilson also demonstrates that birthright membership is not to be equated with tepid or merely formal membership. On the contrary, socialisation to sectarian values via the family often produces the strongest commitment; to leave the sect would mean to embark on a dangerous search for a totally new identity.

Thus we see that neither of Niebuhr's factors—membership through birth rather than choice, and upward social mobility— need prevent a sect from establishing itself as such. Whilst such a sect may have originally developed among those 'suffering strains and tensions differentially experienced within the total society', it may continue as a way of life satisfying to those not significantly deprived of wealth and status. The sect reverses one or more outside values, whether of wealth, patriotism, science or democracy, and it appears that such a reversal can have a continuing appeal. From within it is the world that is eccentric, not the sect, and this is a very understandable viewpoint for those brought up from birth within a socially exclusive sect. Wilson shows that a large proportion of established sect members are born into the group. Yet there are also converts, and small-scale studies of conversion to Mormonism and Jehovah's Witnesses suggest that anomie or social isolation is often a prelude to conversion. The current propaganda of these sects stresses heavily the warmth of social life inside the group, contrasting it with the 'lonely crowd' aspect of life outside. The organisation of meetings and services largely fulfils the propaganda promises. It may be that experience within the group validates the belief in its particular doctrines, which are taken on trust until this experience from within seems to confirm them. A sect which calls for a total commitment from its converts limits its appeal, yet may tie new recruits more closely to it. Their investment of time, energy and loyalty has to be great, and will not lightly be given up. If it is hard to join, it is correspondingly hard to leave. It is also interesting that involvement in a sect is one way of bringing out talents which otherwise remain dormant. Recent accounts of the training programme and assemblies of Jehovah's Witnesses recall accounts of the classes of early Methodist societies, not least in showing how

those previously inarticulate become articulate, those normally
subordinate become leaders.[14]

Nevertheless all studies show that sects have a high death rate.
Few accomplish the transition either to 'established sect' or 'denomination'. But this is not necessarily because the social conditions
favouring sect formation have given way to a more stable or equal
state of society. There may be a high birth rate as well as a high
death rate. But the transience of many sects suggests that there is a
limit to the scale of a sectarian group, especially when it tries to be
a community as well as a worshipping group. Sects show fission
rather than fusion processes, as Clark's book[15] documents for the
American scene, and Wilson's for the British. The cause of fission
often appears as a dispute between rival leaders. Most sects begin as
a group of disciples around a charismatic leader, and there is great
difficulty in adjusting this structure to a larger organisation, and
yet preventing personal loyalties and jealousies from causing
breakaway groups. If the sect develops an authoritarian pattern of
organisation, it may produce revolts against it which lead to new
sectarian offshoots, as the Kilhamites and Primitive Methodists
rebelled against Wesleyan autocracy, or the quarrels of the founders,
Darby and Newton, led to schism within the Brethren. If the sect
concedes, and even emphasises, the autonomy of each congregation,
and allows only fraternal links between them, as Baptists and
Independents have done, some of the congregations will drift into
such diverse theological and ethical positions as to break up the
sect into several different groups, many of which will be too small
to last. The history of the Baptists in England in the eighteenth
century shows this pattern, the extremes being strict and exclusive
Calvinism at one end, and practically a Unitarian position at the
other. American Baptism has shown a multitude of splits, some
based on theological differences, some on moral, some on liturgical
and some on purely personal differences among leaders. Nevertheless, it seems that in favourable circumstances either alternative, of
rigid centralism and hierarchy, or of a loose democracy of congregations, can work effectively up to a size of millions of members.
The Salvation Army shows the first pattern to be feasible, and the
Society of Friends the second.

It is difficult to measure the proportion of sectarianism in a
given society, and not only because of the lack of statistics. To
interpret any figures, we have first to draw a line on the church–
denomination–sect continuum, and this is inevitably a rather
arbitrary procedure. Also a decision has to be taken on what

constitutes a total society, or rather whether the regions or states
for which figures are available constitute total societies. Let us take
an historical example. The Cathari in the context of the whole of
France and Western Christendom were clearly a sect; their beliefs
were heretical on every point and their organisation separate from
the Catholic organisation. Yet in the context of the county of
Toulouse, which for most inhabitants would be the biggest community they knew, the Cathari were so well established, and in such
an overwhelming majority, as to constitute a church rather than a
sect. The same sort of problem arises when estimating the incidence
of sectarianism in tsarist Russia, since many sectarians established
in remote areas parishes or communities beyond the effective reach
of tsarist law. Membership in an 'established sect' such as that of
the Old Believers (originating in the 1660s) might not carry with it
the continuing experience of rejecting and being rejected by society,
because in a very localised world the sectarian group was in effect
the society. It follows that the meaning of an estimate of sectarianism
in eleventh-century France or eighteenth-century Russia is obviously
different from the meaning of such an estimate in modern Britain
or the USA.

Estimates of Dissent in England, which we may take as some
guide to sectarianism, suggest that at the beginning of the nineteenth century it comprised between 5 and 10 % of the population.
This includes the old dissent of Baptists, Congregationalists, Quakers,
Presbyterians and Unitarians, and the new dissent of the Methodists
who had just left the Church of England. These figures suggest a
substantial rise since the mid-eighteenth century, when dissenters
probably accounted for no more than 3 % of the population, and
were to a large extent already moving into a denominational position.
Thus the rise in the second half of the eighteenth century is largely
due to Methodism, although the Baptists were also expanding again.
The sectarian qualities of Methodism, as we shall see, have been
queried, but I include the Methodists here in order to show
the highest possible figure for sectarianism. Clearly this rise in
Dissent coincides with a period of very rapid industrialisation in
England.

A measurement of the position in 1950[16] gives 6·7 % of all those
who acknowledged membership in any religious body belonging to
sects in England and Wales, and 3·9 % in Scotland. This compared
with 72·1 % in churches (Anglican and Roman Catholic) and 21·1 %
in denominations in England and Wales; in Scotland, 88·1 % in
churches (Church of Scotland and Roman Catholic) and 8 % in

denominations. Recent local surveys in England and Wales suggest that sects comprise 4 to 5% of the total population.[17]

The current position in the USA is not very different. In 1947,[18] it was estimated that more than 90% of those affiliated to a religious group belonged to the twenty-four largest churches or denominations. Less than 15% were members of the 400 or more other groups, most of which probably had some sectarian characteristics. However, among these groups there would have been great diversity in the degree of their conflict with the values of the churches and the secular world, the degree of commitment required of their members, and the internal structure of the group.

It is worth recording that in the USA even Catholicism and Judaism have shown some sectarian tendencies; the 'Old Catholic' churches were set up in protest against the 1870 declaration of papal infallibility, and Polish, African and Lithuanian groups seceded on ethnic grounds as well. Reform Judaism was particularly widespread in the USA; it was sectarian in its relation to orthodox Judaism, but rather the reverse in relation to values current in non-Jewish America. Thus its liturgy and theology became more similar to that of liberal Protestantism; it rejected the dietary laws and welcomed modern secular education. Reconstructionism, a very recent development, emphasises Zionism, and a radical reconstruction of Jewish communities in America, and looks forward to the building of a cooperative commonwealth. But it accepts the obligation of dietary and other ritual laws. Thus it is somewhat sectarian in relation to those features of the American way of life which have permeated Judaism.

These very rough figures indicate that in industrial societies, true sects play a very small part, numerically at least. Probably during periods of rapid movement of people—whether into towns or across continents—they play a somewhat larger part. Or, rather, we may say that sects and denominations together play a larger part, as in the frontier society of America and during the British industrial revolution. In the second half of the nineteenth century in England and Wales, Nonconformity was of roughly equal strength with Anglicanism, but clearly nearly all of it was denominational, jealous of Anglican privilege but not hostile to British society, to which it felt a contributor as well as a critic. In other societies, e.g., France and Italy, reformist and revolutionary opinion was mobilised in directly anti-clerical and even anti-religious movements, rather than in sects or denominations. Norway and Sweden represent a third possibility; the official Lutheran churches suffered some loss by the breaking away of 'free church' groups, denominational in character, but were weakened much more by the simple habit of non-participation spreading among all classes.

The major challenge to the churches as the means of salvation has not been from the sects, but from denominations and from anti-clerical movements. The main moral challenge to the churches, in so far as they have been regarded as pillars of an unjust society, has been from secular and political movements. On the fringes of these larger bodies of opinion the sects come and go, providing intense satisfactions to the few but being ignored by the many. They are of various types, and not all would be of the kind Troeltsch described. Some derive more from the middle than from the lower classes. Some are so far removed from any Christian inspiration that they do not come within his category at all, and yet seem similar in social role to those still linked to the Christian tradition. Some of them mix a little religion with a lot of attempted psychotherapy, and therefore do not possess the 'strict ethic' which Troeltsch saw as a distinguishing mark. Finally, neither the introversionist nor the gnostic sects may have that 'passionate hope for the future' which Troeltsch thought to be another characteristic of sects.

In modern usage, in fact, Troeltsch's definition has been widened and simplified. The criterion is that the sect holds religious beliefs which diverge in some aspects radically from those of existing religious groups or of the secular world. Whether the divergence is chiefly on doctrinal, ethical, scientific or political matters, can be left open. Even among the sects of pre-industrial societies with which Troeltsch was concerned, ethical differences were not always to the fore. The Russian Old Believers separated from Orthodoxy on liturgical grounds, and from a distaste for centralised government. The Mormons built up their sect on the basis of a supposed revelation linking the peoples of America with the lost tribes of Israel. Later on the Jehovah's Witnesses based themselves on a particular interpretation of the biblical Book of Revelation, and Christian Science on a scientifically unorthodox view of the relation of mind and matter. Except perhaps in the last case, matters of morality were also involved, but the new group did not simply appeal to the gospel ethic in justifying its particular principles.

I now turn to Martin's claim that not only sects but denominations may break away from the inclusive church, and that in English history the General Baptists, Congregationalists and Methodists represent this kind of secession. The characteristic of a denomination is that it does not make a claim to exclusive possession of religious truth and the means of salvation. It thus concedes toleration to others as well as demanding it for itself. It does not demand from its members total commitment of all aspects of their lives, and does not exercise strict discipline over them. In matters of social ethics, the denomination may be reformist, but it is never revolutionary. Martin argues that from the beginning these were the claims and attitudes of the Baptists, Independents (later Congregationalists) and the Methodists. They differed from the Church of England not in the values they adhered to, but in the effort demanded of their members to practise what all preached. Their organisations drew together all those who were prepared to make this greater moral effort, and this led to strained relations with the more inclusive church. But when the final break with the Church of England took place, this was rather expulsion by the church than an expression of hostility by the denomination.

I find this case hard to accept, because it seems to read back into the debates and quarrels of the seventeenth and eighteenth centuries, an attitude which only grew up in the nineteenth and twentieth. The Independents' leading idea was the 'gathered church', that each group of committed Christians should make its own covenant with God and have the right to call its own pastor, and be subject to no other ecclesiastical authority. This of course was flatly contradictory to Anglican theory and practice. If, as Martin suggests, denominations take a pragmatic view of questions of organisation, then Independents in the seventeenth century were not being denominational. The Baptist condemnation of infant baptism was also put forward as justified by scripture, so that the church practice of infant baptism was condemned outright. In the eighteenth century, Wesley's reluctant ordination of Coke and Astbury represented a direct challenge to the Anglican theory of the priesthood and the position of the bishops. Both sides again defended their view by referring to the Bible. These conflicts were about radical and important disagreements as to the nature of the church in society, matters upon which the Church of England at least could hardly adopt a position of live and let live. Conflicts which, looking back now, may seem insignificant compared with the range of similar or identical values had a very different perspective to the contestants. That the disagreements seemed very important to church and state is surely shown by the severity of laws against Nonconformists in 1660, and the persistence of their civil disabilities well into the nineteenth century. When we consider that the idea of religious toleration was hardly born in the seventeenth century, and that all rulers believed firmly that religious unity was necessary to social order, it seems a misnomer to call any separated religious group in that century a denomination. Martin is, of course, correct in quoting a few English Dissenters of that period in favour of religious toleration, but this opinion was so radically at odds with the ruling opinions of the day that it could, and did, appear as a threat to social order rather than a recipe for social peace.

Admittedly Methodism in the eighteenth century grew up in quite a different context from that of Independent and Baptist groups over a century earlier. The idea and practice of toleration had gained a great deal of ground. Even so, Wesleyanism aroused enormous hostility and jealousy in Anglican circles, which all its professions of loyalty to church and king could not allay. Furthermore from Wesleyan Methodism there sprang the Kilhamite and Primitive Methodists, and later the Bible Christians, which all had democratic and radical tendencies. If the willingness to tolerate others is the chief mark of denominationalism, then the Methodists were denominational from the start. But if the main criterion is that the group is tolerated because its values and practices do not diverge much from those of the church, then Methodism, at the beginning of its independent life, was sectarian.

Reverting to the analysis of sectarianism in the strict sense, I would like to refer to the work of Hobsbawm[19] and Cohn,[20] the one adopting a Marxist approach and the other a Freudian. Both are concerned with what Wilson has termed adventist sects, those which look forward to a second coming of Christ, to the establishment, by divine intervention, of the Kingdom of Heaven on earth. Hobsbawm, following in the wake of Engels' interpretation of primitive Christianity and the German Peasants' War, studied heretical religious movements in Europe, and tried to show how they were connected with rebellion against class oppression. Thus he assembles evidence to show that millennialism was endemic in Andalusian society in the nineteenth century, and led eventually to the growth of syndicalist workers' unions. He shows how millennialist fervour was active against the crown and the bourgeoisie during the English civil war and its aftermath, and how medieval sects, whilst prophesying that the millennium was at hand, did not remain passive, but actively attacked wealth and privilege. These examples fit in with the hypothesis that sects of the adventist or millennialist type are pre-political, and form a necessary prelude to directly political action. They represent the first awakening of protest, the first realisation that something other than patient resignation is possible, and the first lessons in class organisation. There is a kind of trial-and-error process from sectarian utopianism to realistic secular movements, such as political parties and trade unions. (This view is similar to Worsley's interpretation of Melanesian millennial sects—see Chapter 3.)

Cohn's work is a more comprehensive study of medieval millennial sects than Hobsbawm's group of case studies, and from it he draws different conclusions. He sees millennialism as the response of men driven to such desperation that they are in a pathological mental state, and in consequence act irrationally. The pathos of their movements is their inevitable failure; millennial visions do not solve the problems which beset hungry peasants or exploited artisans. After the prophecy has failed, the disappointed sectary falls back into apathy, or looks for another version of the same kind of message of divine intervention. In either case, no development to a more rational strategy of protest need occur. Cohn stresses the ephemeral nature of millennial sects in the Middle Ages, the lack of any clear political sequel to them. He draws an analogy with modern Fascist movements, which he regards also as products of mental disorder, and as also unable to fulfil their promise of heaven on earth. He thinks that such ideologies, whether couched in religious or secular terms, are so far removed from reality that they cannot be effective means of tackling the true sources of deprivation and frustration. Nor is there, to his mind, any evidence of the trial-and-error process by which religious millennial movements are closely succeeded by more effective political protests. They are rather sporadic outbursts occasioned by some worsening of social conditions, as for instance when bad harvests or epidemics or ravaging armies threaten traditional subsistence agriculture. So far as millennial visions emboldened men to attack their rulers, or the rich, e.g., by burning evidence of indebtedness, or by looting and murder, these purely destructive gestures did nothing but relieve feelings, and formed a barrier rather than a beginning to more rational activities.

Cohn's criticism of the Marxist interpretation of Christian millennial sects seems to me convincing. However, his view that sectaries were mentally disturbed seems impossible to establish; evidence is necessarily lacking. It might be so, but it seems unlikely; at least in relation to the medieval and sixteenth- and seventeenth-century sects. Given that during these centuries nearly all thinking about society was carried out in religious categories, that the authority of the Bible was widely accepted, and that apocalyptic expectations could be supported from scripture (the Book of Revelation, and Daniel in particular), it cannot be argued that millennial beliefs are in themselves evidence of mental illness (if that concept has any meaning, cross-culturally!). It is clear that even today, when non-religious categories are available to the social critic, and the authority of the Bible widely discounted, members of adventist sects are by no means mentally unbalanced in the common-sense usage of this term.

In relation to both the Marxist and the Freudian theses, it is as well to remember that millennial beliefs in Christian history have cropped up from time to time in quite exalted social circles. It is not only the deprived and oppressed of a given age who feel so radically that the times are out of joint. Rulers faced with uncontrollable disorders or natural disasters, or morally sensitive members of a ruling class, may also cast their fears and hopes into an apocalyptic mould. This suggests that it is inadequate to view such beliefs solely as means, rational or irrational, by which the poor and lowly wage their battle against the rich and powerful. The expressive aspect of these movements needs also to be taken into account. When we do this, we notice that millennial beliefs can be associated with the actual construction of a more perfectly Christian community. The vision of the future is translated, albeit on a tiny scale, into present actuality. Millennialism has not transformed whole states, but has sometimes been the midwife of such miniature communities of Christian charity.

1. E. Troeltsch, *The Social Teachings of the Christian Churches,* p. 993.

2. ibid., pp. 993–4.

3. ibid., p. 996.

4. ibid., p. 994.

5. ibid., p. 1001.

6. ibid., p. 1004.

7. W. Stark, *Sociology of Religion: A Study of Christendom,* 1966.

8. H. R. Niebuhr, *Social Sources of Denominationalism,* 1954.

9. W. Herberg, *Protestant, Catholic, Jew,* 1960.

10. B. Wilson, *Sects and Society,* 1961.
    —*Patterns of Sectarianism,* 1967.

11. D. A. Martin, 'The Denomination', *British Journal of Sociology,* vol. XII, 1962.

12. B. Wilson, *Patterns of Sectarianism,* p. 31.

13. ibid., p. 45.

14. R. Brandon, 'Jehovah's Witnesses', *New Society*, 7 August 1969.

15. E. T. Clark, *The Small Sects in America*, 1949.

16. J. Highet, 'Scottish Religious Adherence', *British Journal of Sociology*, vol. IV, 1953.

17. From surveys quoted in L. Paul, *The Payment and Development of the Clergy*, 1964.

18. E. T. Clark, op. cit.

19. E. Hobsbawm, *Primitive Rebels*, 1959.

20. N. Cohn, *Pursuit of the Millennium*, 1957.

6

CHURCH AND STATE

The terms 'church' and 'state' are only useful to the discussion of religion in large-scale complex societies, where the differentiation of social institutions has proceeded a long way. Even so, it may be argued that they import into the comparative study of religious organisation a typology drawn only from the limited experience of Christendom. (As we have seen, a similar criticism may be made of the terms 'sect' and 'denomination'.) Nevertheless, I propose to use these terms in a preliminary analysis of the relations of religious and political institutions in Christian states and societies. From this analysis some questions will arise which lend themselves to comparative study. Since Islam and Buddhism are similar to Christianity in being strongly missionary religions, and therefore transcending state boundaries, I propose to limit comparisons to these three cases.

Troeltsch's definition of the church as a comprehensive and therefore compromising type of Christian religious organisation has already been introduced. But, as he himself emphasised, the church can be comprehensive, and yet have varying relations with the political order. He identified three such relationships: the imperial church, in which church and state were coterminous and mutually supportive; the territorial churches, in which the religious organisation was part of the fragmented feudal organisation of society, and largely subordinate to secular leaders; and the papal church, in which a unified ecclesiastical hierarchy confronted the various independent European states.

Troeltsch's classification refers chiefly to the pre-Reformation history of Western Christianity; Stark's definitions of 'established' and 'universal' churches refers largely to the post-Reformation period and to Eastern Orthodoxy, which Troeltsch leaves out of his account. If we extend Troeltsch's classification into the later period, we find territorial churches to be the dominant type, in Orthodoxy, Catholicism and Protestantism. Yet, as the territorial unit of sovereignty has been enlarged since the feudal era, so the territorial church organised within the boundaries of the state has also become larger. Within this group of territorial churches it would be possible to use Stark's typology of 'universal' and 'established' churches, provided we recognise many intermediary positions between these two extremes. Churches within the Catholic fold, in which there is some recognition of papal claims over all believers, no matter what their citizenship, would be treated as branches of a 'universal' church, whereas churches such as the Anglican and Lutheran during the sixteenth to eighteenth centuries would lie near to the established church type, since in those cases there was little or no institutional recognition of the unity of membership across state boundaries. However, it is doubtful whether such a classification, attempted for the whole of the post-Reformation period, would rightly assign all the territorial branches of Roman Catholicism to the category of 'universal', and place all Protestant churches near the extreme of 'establishment'. Stark himself points out the initial effort of Calvinism to transcend state frontiers and establish a new 'universal' church. The recent history of Lutheranism and Anglicanism shows a number of attempts at international organisation, and efforts to demonstrate the world-wide character of Protestant Christianity. These efforts are partly the consequence of European expansion and missionary enterprise, partly a witness to the ecumenical spirit, and they therefore produce a result very different from the hierarchical organisation of Catholicism, with its long centuries of papal tradition and its stress on the priestly function. Yet, taken together, they represent a move away from the 'established' church position of earlier times. On the other hand, a detailed examination of church-state relations in Catholic countries since the Reformation would show, at least for certain important states, considerable inroads by the secular ruler into the 'universal' character of the church. In France Gallicanism, and in Austria Josephism, limited the independent action of the pope as head of the Church.

An attempt to classify the relations of churches to states on these lines would overlook one most important feature of the post-Reformation age, the emergence of states professedly secular, or at least tolerant of other religions than the one traditionally established. Even granting Stark's full thesis of the radical distinction between the 'universal' church of Catholicism and the 'established' Church of Anglicanism, it is obvious that the position of the Catholic Church *vis-à-vis* the state in France was greatly changed by the introduction of religious tolerance and state control after the Revolution of 1789, just as the position of Anglicanism was altered by the gradual establishment of religious toleration in Britain and by the spread of Anglicanism overseas. Thus even within the limited history of Western Christian states, at least two further types of relationship between state and religious institutions can be traced. There have arisen states practising religious tolerance and accepting religious pluralism and religious indifference, for example, contemporary Switzerland, Britain, France, West Germany and the USA, and there are states which have attempted a thoroughgoing secularisation in respect of all traditional faiths, such as the Communist states of Eastern Europe, and, rather more hesitantly, Nazi Germany. To examine the social conditions permitting the emergence of the two latter types of relation between political and religious organisation is a task beyond the scope of this book; I think, however, that such an examination would reveal two contrasting backgrounds. At one extreme there is the rise of a vehement Nationalist or Communist movement, which suspects all alternative centres of loyalty and organisation, particularly religious ones asserting equally absolute but conflicting values. Soviet Russia and the German National Socialist state are examples of this type. At the other extreme there is the emergence of a state, national or multi-national, in which bargaining and compromise between more or less organised interests, religious, regional, economic or linguistic, is the norm, and a degree of dissensus is expected. Britain, the USA and modern India approximate to this position. The religious toleration entrenched in the American constitution was not just the expression of the deism of the eighteenth-century Enlightenment; it was the necessary consequence of federating thirteen colonies of different religious foundations. The growth of toleration in Britain can be seen as the gradual yielding of Anglicanism to the growing social and economic power of Nonconformity and Catholicism within the framework of a relatively liberal form of parliamentary government. The case of France after 1789 is particularly interesting, for the immediate fervour of Nationalism and anti-clericalism after the revolution, together with the attempted cult of Reason, show similarities with the religious policies of Fascist or Communist states. But Napoleon's religious settlement bears much more the character of a compromise with established religious groups, not an attempt to supersede them. Toleration was granted to all, and thereby some religious hindrances to national unity removed. All groups were to be under surveillance by the state, so that they could not set up in competition with it. Modern France is an example of a state practising toleration, and accepting religious indifference and pluralism, but this outcome of the turbulent political history since 1789 is the result of the balance of power between contrasting parties and opinions; there have always been ardent partisans of a Christian Catholic Nationalism, and equally strong supporters of a National-ism based on the three revolutionary absolutes—Liberty, Equality, Fraternity.

The group of states which are institutionally secular and religiously tolerant contrast strongly with those based on one 'secular' political creed, held as absolutely true and expressed in ritual. I think that for a ruling group to maintain the first position and not slide into the second is a difficult task. If religious toleration is possible because rulers rely on national sentiment for their legitimacy, there is always the risk that Nationalism itself may develop into a religion intolerant of others. Movements such as McCarthyism in the USA in the 1950s, the British Union of Fascists in the 1930s, and Action Française during the same period, show how easily Nationalism can become the basis of intolerance and quasi-religious fervour. What was incipient and controllable in Britain, France and the USA, became dominant in Hitler's Germany, where the patriotism of the élite was outbid by the extreme Nationalism of a mass movement.

The other frequent support of religious toleration has been the anti-clericalism of workers' movements in industrial Europe. This can be seen in Protestant Scandinavia as much as in Catholic France or Italy. These workers' movements have usually absorbed some elements of Marxism, in which case they may become anti-religious, not only anti-clerical. Marxist movements in power have developed what to all non-Marxists is an alternative religion, i.e., the ritual celebration of absolute values and historical forces, and have in general been intolerant of traditional religions. It would seem that, as in the case of Nationalism, what has been a prop of religious tolerance may turn into its opposite. However, since no Communist Party has yet come to power without external support in a tradi-tionally tolerant secular state, this prediction cannot be tested. The nearest case is that of Yugoslavia, whose Communist regime has been fairly tolerant except in the case of the Catholic Church, where complicating factors of Nationalism and wartime collaboration with the German forces come into play.

Christian experience in general suggests that until very recent times all rulers sought to legitimate their authority in religious terms and found it quite possible to do this even while limiting the claims of the church upon them, or supporting some new variant of the old ecclesiastical authorities. Nevertheless in the West there were two periods in which the church was very powerful on its own account. The first was during the Germanic invasions of the Western Roman Empire from the fourth to the sixth century A.D. Here the bishops and monks appeared as the representatives of a higher civilisation, as heirs to imperial Rome, as the essential helpers of barbarian chiefs striving to set up kingdoms in their newly won territories. Ecclesiastics helped some of them to success, and in so doing eventually diminished their own power. In the second period, the High Middle Ages of the thirteenth and fourteenth centuries, the church had better survived the fragmentation of authority of the feudal age, or emerged earlier from it, than had the lay political leaders, the kings and princes. Hence the church could act as a power among the powers, allied now with one, now with another, subordinate to none though never able to impose its will on all. Since the end of the Middle Ages, the power of the church has waned, and with it the Catholic vision of Christian unity. And no other church has arisen to embody that vision more successfully. Yet whatever the balance of power between church and lay ruler, we see this recurrent claim of such rulers to religious legitimation of their limited authority, coupled with the persistence of a theoretic universalism in the creed and moral code of the church or churches whose blessing they seek. Until the recent rise of Nationalism and Communism all political claims were made in Christian terms, and religious unity within the state was conceived as essential to the effective wielding of political power. Even Nationalism has been as often allied with some version of Christianity as opposed to it, as the examples of Ireland, Poland, Spain and the Netherlands indicate. Why then has the universalist aspect of Christianity persisted, why has not Christianity been completely reduced to the status of a group religion? The answer, I think, lies in those structural aspects of large-scale literate societies which encourage the proclamation of one God in whose worship all can and should join. If we take the three cases in which this message has formed the basis of a new religious system, Buddhism, Christianity and Islam, we find at the beginning individuals who were profoundly dissatisfied with the society in which they found themselves, and who proclaimed their message to others of like mind, with whom a new community could be established. In terms of ethic and emotion, their gospels were about persons, regardless of their group affiliations. (This generalisation requires some qualification in respect of Mohammed and Islam, as we shall show in the subsequent discussion of this religion.) Their message had universal application because it spoke to individuals and formed the basis for new forms of community, but the universalism was derived from the appeal to individuals and the critique of existing society, not from a philosophically based repudiation of polytheism, nor from any goal of universal empire. It seems likely that such tension between individual and society, such dissatisfaction with all social roles, will arise only in large-scale societies, in which change and migration are common, and in which trade breaks up communal ties and induces new forms of social inequality. But it is also likely that only in such large-scale societies will there arise the comparison and criticism of cults, myths and beliefs, a free-ranging intellectual enterprise that will develop a theoretic monotheism, or at least, as in the case of Buddhism, a devastating belittling of the power of traditional gods and devils.

In the case of Christianity a link was soon forged between the individualist gospel of Jesus, allied originally with Jewish monotheism, and the speculative theism of Greek philosophy. This link was only possible when the ritual ties of Jewish monotheism to specifically Jewish tradition and history were cut; the individualist emphasis of Jesus' teaching enabled this to be done.

I put forward these two conditions of social structure and intellectual development as basic to the emergence of a universalist religion. But there is a third condition most important for its successful propagation, and that is its appeal to political leaders who are trying to unify and rule over a large-scale society. The universal religion cuts across existing cults which express the loyalties of small groups and localities. If it can be super-imposed on these cults, still better if it can be substituted for them, the ruler sees his task of unification eased. Thus the Roman emperors first tried to establish their own cult as an expression of loyalty by their subjects; later they managed practically to merge the cults of emperor, of the sun and of Christ, and to claim legitimacy on this new religious basis. Of course in such a merger the truly universal character of Christianity was modified; henceforth it would be, in one aspect, only the religion of the Roman Empire. But because this

imperial society still possessed those social and intellectual characteristics which had allowed Christianity to be proclaimed and to take
root, there continued to be new outbreaks of that individualist form
of religion of which primitive Christianity was the prototype, and
which revived its idealistic and universal aspects. Stressing the
contents of the gospel rather than the social conditions in which its
message is received, Troeltsch makes the same point when he refers
to the continuing potential for sectarian and mystical interpretations
of Christianity.

It is important to remember that, as in the earliest days, religious
idealism expressed itself in missionary enterprise. This of course
was now much more compounded with politics than in the days of
Paul and his successors, but it was never merely the religious aspect
of conquest or of the spread of a technologically superior civilisation.
The missionaries were ahead of the armies, even if they welcomed
their eventual help. Since more and more communities were brought
into the fold of Christianity, although the Empire was no longer
strong enough to incorporate them politically, Christianity was not
reduced completely to a group religion, or a series of group religions,
though that fate was sometimes perilously near. The Christian
message appealed particularly to those rulers, whether of German,
Hun or Slav origin, who were trying to establish large kingdoms in
new territories; here the political attractiveness of a universal
religion to rulers of new and enlarged states combined with the
work of the missionaries fired with their message of salvation and
brotherhood. It has often been said that the product was only a
veneer of Christianity overlaying a vast mass of folk religion and
magic. Yet this metaphor of veneer is ill-chosen. The Christian
element in this compound of religion and magic linked one state
with another, and often helped the construction of larger units. It
enabled the penetration of many different communities by a body
of men versed in a single literature and philosophy, and thereby
gave some cultural unity to Christendom. Among these men were
the monks, who established new forms of community, and thus
attracted in each generation some of those who wished most keenly
to revive the primitive Christian ethics. I think it no coincidence that
only the three universalist religions have developed monasticism.
Only by renouncing property, and the family ties which are used so
often to justify the search for property and power, can a truly new
start in human relations be made, a new example given to the world.
The conviction that such a fresh start needs to be made arises from
that increased tension between individual and group which derives

from the structure of a large and diverse society with its apparently insoluble moral dilemmas at the political level.

Wach, in his book *Sociology of Religion*,[1] also links the development of large polities with the maintenance of universalist religion, though he believes the original emergence of such religions to be inexplicable. He treats the question of church-state relations in terms of three stages, the first of which is the primitive identity of religious and political community. At the second stage there is a development of 'cultic organisation' separate from political and administrative institutions, but 'neither state nor religion is universal in principle at this stage. They always bear together a regional, ethnic or national character.'[2] The third stage is 'characterised by a high degree of political development and an insistent claim for universality on the part of the religious community'.[3] This seems a useful categorisation, so long as we insert two provisos. The first is that the 'insistent claim for universality on the part of the religious community' can be very much muted by the equally insistent claim of kings that they in particular have received the mandate of heaven. Nevertheless, so far as rulers are concerned, it is clear that they welcome legitimation in terms of a universal God, rather than in terms of one of lower standing, and in that way they reinforce universalism. But in so far as they use their faith in the service of power politics, they help to give Christianity that 'regional, ethnic or national character' which Wach attributes to religions of the pre-universal stage. The Christian God becomes the God of the Byzantines, the Franks or the Spaniards, and loses his universalism in practice if not in theory. In fact there seems so much inevitable oscillation between Wach's second and third stages that it is doubtful whether 'stage', with its connotation of temporal progress, is an apt word to use. Yet Wach is surely right in asserting that universalism in principle, once reached, is never given up.

The second proviso to his generalisation refers to the supposed role of the religious community. If we take this, in the example of Christianity, to refer to the whole body of Christians, it is obvious that they have not made an 'insistent claim for universality', but have rather been preoccupied with ways by which a universal God can be brought to attend to the fears and hopes of particular groups, whether families, villages, or countries. Subjects, as much as rulers, have helped to domesticate Christian belief to the support of particular groups and mundane aims. If Wach's 'religious community' means, as is more likely, the group of religious specialists, for example, the ecclesiastical hierarchy in Catholic Christianity, there still remain difficulties about the 'insistence of their claim to universality'. When the Western Church was feudalised, ecclesiastical positions were necessarily filled mostly by those clerics who best played the game of treating their positions as pieces of private property. Such men were hardly champions of a universal religion. In fact the insistence on universality has often come from the fringes of the church establishment, or even beyond it, from reforming monks, and from those, churchmen or sectarians, who tried to go back to the small-scale congregational Christianity of primitive times. In adding this qualification to Wach's statement I hope to emphasise again the essential paradox of belief in a universal God who is both powerful and loving. As a God of power he appeals particularly to rulers of large and diversified societies; as a God of love he appeals most to the sensitive and gentle who wish to escape from the injustice and violence inseparable from such societies. The latter proclaim him, but the former take up his cause, and thereby transform it.

Several of the features found in Christian experience of church and state have their parallels in Buddhist history. The Buddha perhaps withdrew more dramatically from political society than did Jesus, but he returned more completely to it. He and his immediate disciples were already the advisers of kings. The spread of Buddhism, as of Christianity, was rapid, and the adoption of it by Asoka, the great Indian empire-builder, can be compared with the official adoption of Christianity by the Roman Empire. Again the more universalist religion is favoured by the most powerful ruler. The Asokan Empire was shorter-lived than the Roman, nevertheless we can see that subsequent efforts by Indian princes to build large-scale polities were usually accompanied by favours shown to Buddhism. Some of the most successful of these political endeavours were made by non-Indian invaders from Asia Minor or Central Asia; it seems likely that Buddhism had the attraction for them which Christianity had for Germanic and Slav rulers in Europe, that it was a universal religion overarching local and caste loyalties. The spread of Buddhism to Ceylon during the reign of Asoka, and its subsequent consolidation as the religion of the people during the struggles against Hindu kingdoms in South India, calls to mind such parallels as the conversion of the Franks and their role of champions of Christianity against pagans and Moslems. Burma is another case where the building of a large-scale state went hand in hand with the effective establishment of the universal religion of Buddhism. In both the Burmese and the Ceylonese cases there was also the attraction to the native ruler of contact with a powerful and advanced civilisation professing that religion; this also was a favourable element in the advance of Christianity in Europe.

A third case in which Buddhism spread to a more primitive people is that of Tibet, and here again there is the phenomenon of a ruler engaged in constructing a large polity enthusiastically adopting a universal religion. The way in which monasteries became the centres of social organisation, in which abbots began to rival and even dominate the lay nobility, surely owes something to this circumstance of the relative primitiveness of pre-Buddhist Tibetan society. Again there is a parallel from early Christendom, in the monastic domination of Celtic Christianity.

Buddhism came to Japan via China and Korea, again as part of a superior civilisation. But Confucian ideas travelled to Japan at the same time, and it is interesting to see that the Japanese prince, who in the seventh century A.D. for the first time unified the islands under one ruler, enthusiastically accepted both doctrines. There followed a good deal of syncretism between the native Shinto worship of nature gods and Confucian and Buddhist cults. But Buddhism gained the most in official patronage, and by a division of religious labours peculiar to Japan, has coexisted with Shinto through the centuries. Like Christianity in Europe, it was sometimes given a particularly patriotic interpretation, but it was also the source of idealistic and truly universal sects which stressed the individual's need for enlightenment and salvation.

Only in China did Buddhism come to a country as advanced in civilisation as the India of its origin, and already unified politically. In these circumstances it is not surprising that Confucian rites and doctrines continued to provide legitimacy for the emperor, while Buddhism remained unestablished and mostly without state patronage. Like the various Taoist schools, the Buddhist monasteries could attract those dissatisfied with the Confucian sanctification of traditional social forms of family and empire. Buddhism and Taoism together played a part similar to Christian sects and orders in focussing and expressing religious enthusiasms of a more individualist and therefore universal character. The main schools of Chinese Buddhism, the Pure Land Sect and Chan Buddhism (equivalent to the Japanese Zen), are very different from one another, but have in common their concern with the fate of the individual, not that of the state or nation.

In spite of the various suggestive parallels of Buddhist and Christian states, there has been one great differentiating factor, and that is the absence in Buddhism of any hierarchical structure of religious personnel claiming obedience in some respects from all the faithful. The 'samgha', the Buddhist community, might refer to a single monastery and its body of lay adherents, or to groups of monasteries united by owning a single founder or a special variant of doctrine or ritual. Such groups might exist within or across the boundaries of states, but not even the largest such group approximated the unified hierarchical structure of the Catholic Church, with its pyramid of parish priests, bishops and metropolitans, culminating in the papacy. And even in a country like Ceylon or Burma, where Buddhism supports and is supported by state power and national feeling, the 'samgha' has not the same hierarchic, even bureaucratic, structure as in state-supported Lutheran or Orthodox Churches. This great difference in the religious institutions of Buddhism and Christianity is probably linked with the fact that wars of religion and persecution of heretics have been much rarer in Buddhist than in Christian countries, even where Buddhism has worn a political character.

Buddhism appeared as a variant of Hinduism, and Christianity of Judaism. The third great universal and missionary religion, Islam, appeared as an Arabian adaptation of Christianity and Judaism. But whereas Buddhism and Christianity were born and developed in the centres of civilisation, Indian and Graeco–Roman, Islam originated on the fringe of two civilisations, the Persian and the Byzantine. Its prophet, Mohammed, borrowed from the theism of Christianity and Judaism in an effort to reform and unify an Arabian society half tribal, half urban and commercial. Therefore his ethical teaching was not to withdraw from traditional society and begin afresh by constructing new small congregations of the faithful, but thoroughly to reform traditional society, and enlarge its scale by eliminating tribal rivalries. Thus from the very beginning of Islam its leaders were attempting to build a polity and a religious community of equal scale, whereas Christian and Buddhist rulers were adapting a congregational religion to their wider political needs. In terms of 'church-state' relations, Mohammed and his immediate successors were struggling with the same sort of problems that Christian Roman or barbarian rulers such as Justinian or Charlemagne had faced in the West. They were all using universalist religion in the same sort of way, as a means of unification and a carrier of all the civilised arts of the day. As the Arabs, unified in their new faith, speedily made vast territorial conquests, the problems of organising a much wider and more diverse body of the faithful (and the unconverted) multiplied. Mohammed's simple prescriptions of brotherhood and sharing of war booty no longer sufficed, any more than the Sermon on the Mount provided adequate guidance to Christian rulers. As in Christianity, internal splits and quarrels multiplied, with regional, cultural and class conflicts reappearing as religious differences. In spite of the fact that at the beginning the universalism of Islam was expressed more in terms of large-scale political enterprise than in terms of a search for the means of individual salvation, this latter aspect was soon to come to the fore. From the second century of Islam the 'sufi' orders multiplied. These groups were like the congregations of primitive Christianity, or the monastic orders of Buddhism and Christianity, in that they were specifically religious groups, aiming at salvation for the individual, and often with a missionary purpose besides. Sometimes the groups, like monks, were set apart physically from society. Thus in Islam too there emerged a powerful expression of salvation-religion, alongside the repeated endeavours of rulers to establish a theocratic state.

Despite the existence of the 'sufi' orders, and of specialists in religious tradition and sacred law, Islam displays, even less than Buddhism, institutions similar to those of the Christian churches. The 'sufis' never, and the legal specialists rarely, exercised the sort of social authority which Buddhist abbots or Christian bishops have frequently done. The 'ulema', the legal specialists, had various centres of influence, but no unified structure throughout Moslem society. A priesthood never developed because the liturgical simplicity of Islam never required one. The ultimate form of legitimacy for a Moslem ruler was to pronounce himself caliph, the representative and successor to Mohammed, but there was never any similarity between the position of caliph and pope, and since A.D. 750 no caliph has been able to legitimate his position with all Moslem communities. Whether caliphs or no, Moslem rulers have generally sought to legitimate their actions in terms of a comprehensive body of sacred law. But Islamic states, like Christian ones, have been challenged by secular Nationalism and Socialism, as in Iran, Turkey, and the modern Arab states. In these cases the conflict is centred on the content and source of laws, not on the status of particular groups of religious specialists. What the Nationalists and Socialists demand, and have sometimes obtained, is a denial of the authority of the sacred law over modern law-makers, a removal of the last remnant of the original theocratic enterprise.

Finally we must note that there has been much variety in the

practice of Moslem rulers with regard to the toleration and assimilation of non-Moslem subjects. In spite of the theocratic tendencies
of orthodoxy, there have been rulers such as Akbar the Great in
Mogul India who not only tolerated the Hinduism of millions of
his subjects, but tried to legitimate his authority by the creation of
a new syncretic religion reconciling Islam with Hinduism.

In trying to show the sociological connections of universal
faiths with both small-scale congregational religion and large-scale
polities I have stressed chiefly the similarities of the three faiths of
Buddhism, Christianity and Islam. I should therefore perhaps add a
word of warning that this treatment is necessarily incomplete, and
does not do justice to many unique aspects of each religious system.

1. J. Wach, *Sociology of Religion*, 1947, ch. VII.
2. ibid., p. 304.
3. ibid., p. 314.

7

WEBER'S SOCIOLOGY OF RELIGION

Weber's famous essay on *The Protestant Ethic and the Spirit of Capitalism* was published in 1904,[1] quite early in his career as economic historian and sociologist. In this, his first venture into the sociology of religion, Weber tackles the problem of the relation between religious beliefs and practical ethics, particularly the ethics of economic activity, in Western society from the sixteenth century to the present day. This problem, in the context of different religions and civilisations, remained his chief interest, and his studies of ancient Judaism, and of the religions of India and China, as well as of Graeco–Roman religion and sectarian Christianity, are all related to it. Nevertheless, though this question of economic ethics provided a focus, his field ranged very widely over the whole field of possible relations between types of society and types of religion. To follow his line of thought, the simplest way in which to begin is to analyse the argument of the essay on the Protestant ethic, and then to see how this led him on to comparative studies of other religions and other social structures.

His first task is to present the evidence for an association between certain forms of Protestantism and a speedy advance towards capitalism. He draws on the familiar example of the Netherlands in the sixteenth and seventeenth centuries, of the relative shares in capitalist enterprise of Huguenots and Catholics in France in the sixteenth and seventeenth centuries, of the English Puritans, and above all of that branch of English Puritanism which settled in America and constituted New England. He is primarily interested in these examples because they represent the occasions where the new attitudes to economic activity dramatically broke up the old economic traditionalism. Weber's view was that such a rejection of tradition, such a rapid change in the method and valuation of economic activity, could not have occurred without a moral and religious driving force. But he also adduces evidence of a continuing difference in the way that different religious groups participated in the established capitalism of his own day. In Germany, France and Hungary, he claims that the distribution of occupations and the educational preparation for them shows that Protestants of a Calvinistic persuasion are more likely to take entrepreneurial and managerial roles, and to take up work in modern large-scale organisations, than are Catholics or Lutheran Protestants. These latter tend to remain in farming, in the ranks of small-scale artisan enterprises, or in humanistic professions such as law and administration.

Having established this correlation between Calvinistic Protestantism and capitalism, Weber goes on to try and identify the distinguishing features of modern capitalism as against other types of economic organisation, and the distinguishing features of Calvininism as against other versions of Christianity. On the first point, he is not arguing that the pioneers of capitalism were more acquisitive or greedier than their predecessors in non-capitalist society, nor that these latter didn't realise that the road to wealth lay through accumulation of capital. More than once he explicitly says 'capitalistic acquisition as an adventure has been at home in all types of economic society which have known trade with the use of money, and which have offered opportunities through *commenda*, farming of taxes, state loans, financing of wars, ducal courts and office-holders. Likewise the inner attitude of the adventurer, which laughs at all ethical limitations, has been universal.'[2] But he is very certain that this 'adventure capitalism' or 'political capitalism' is quite different from the careful calculation of profit and loss in a regular and continuing enterprise, which is the typical activity of the modern capitalist. The latter does not need the state, except as a guardian of that law and order which permits him to be methodical and rational in the conduct of his business. He does not rely on the state, as his predecessors did, either as a source of privileges and monopolies, or as a borrower whose shortage of cash can be a source of great, if risky, profit to him. Moreover, whilst in the pre-capitalistic society the activities of the trader and financier were at least suspect, and at worst subject to severe condemnation by the church and popular opinion, the pioneers of modern capitalism saw a positive ethical and religious value in their work, and tended to see the wealth in which it resulted as God's blessing on their mode of life. The participant in modern capitalism, whether as entrepreneur, manager or labourer, was, according to Weber, by no means just a deviant from a tradition which hindered technical and organisational change, and reprobated new accumulation of wealth; he was a believer in the ethic of hard work, of systematic improvement of means to the end of greater production and trade, of frugality in personal consumption, and of individual rather than collective responsibility in economic life. How was this new evaluation of work and thrift related to Protestantism? In Weber's view the doctrine of the 'calling' was the essential basis of the new values, and the doctrine of predestination engendered the will-power necessary to put them into practice. He makes, I think, a strong case for the view that Protestants were encouraged to think of their everyday work, in whatever occupation, as a means by which they should glorify God. Their work should be undertaken with the same seriousness and sense of duty as the Catholic monk was encouraged to bring to bear in his special 'calling'. Work was an intrinsic value, not just a consequence of the curse of Adam. It would also, I think, be agreed that Calvinism rather than Catholicism or Lutheranism emphasised the freedom to choose a calling, rather than the obligation to accept that to which one was born. These two aspects of the doctrine of the calling, seriousness in work, and individual right and duty to choose a field of activity, would clearly contribute to economic advance if they were not merely preached, but actually practised. Weber believes that they were largely practised wherever the Calvinist doctrine of predestination took effective hold. This dogma was presented by Calvinists as a logical deduction from the omnipotence of God and the sinfulness of man. In justice, all men merited eternal damnation; but God in his mercy had, through Christ, chosen some for salvation. But no man could know God's eternal decrees which pre-ordained salvation or damnation. All men must nevertheless struggle to obey God's commandments on this earth, without preoccupation with their own state of election or reprobation. 'The chief end of man is to glorify God', says the Calvinist confession of faith, and this was a commandment to all. Weber readily agrees that this doctrine did not suddenly appear as an intellectual construction, without social antecedents. It was in fact worked out in debate with Catholics and Lutherans, as an attack on sacramental Christianity, the consequent power of the priesthood, and the moral corruption to which the doctrine of salvation by works had seemed to lead. Weber, however, is not interested in these reasons why Calvinism should have developed, but in the changes it wrought in those who adopted it. He traces the ways in which Calvinists sought, despite the austere teachings of their founder, to attain certainty of their own salvation. They accepted from him that there could be no return to the sacraments, to confession and absolution, yet they needed some salve for their anxiety. Consequently, they found in ceaseless activity, in strong self-discipline, and in methodical pursuit of their aims, a reassurance that they were indeed among the elect. If doubts arose, they could be stilled by a further application of the same medicine. But the doubts had to be quieted, the assurance gained, by the individual himself. No friend, no priest, no church could guarantee him, or help him towards, a state of grace. Weber admits that the doctrine of predestination could, and did in the case of seventeenth-century Jansenism in France, lead to an ethic of quietism and contemplation rather than to an increase in worldly activity. In fact he notes that Pascal, a leading Jansenist, interprets both acquisitiveness and asceticism as means by which men trick themselves into forgetting their own sinfulness, and commit thereby the further sin of spiritual pride. Yet he argues that it is equally natural and consistent for a belief in predestination to be the springboard for a systematic and disciplined active life in the world, for, to use his own phrase, the adoption of 'inner-worldly asceticism'. Thus, given that the possibility of capitalist development was more or less equally available to all countries in sixteenth-century Europe, it was no accident that the possibilities were actualised only among the Calvinistic Protestants of the Netherlands, England, New England, France, Switzerland and parts of Germany.

Weber acknowledges that the full rigour of Calvinist doctrines was soon softened within the Reformed churches, but he equally emphasises that there were also revivals of Calvinistic ideas, such as Pietism in seventeenth-century Germany, and Calvinist Baptism in England and America in the same period, and finally Wesleyan Methodism in eighteenth-century Britain. Since these movements were never so wholeheartedly Calvinist in theology and ethics as the original Calvinist Reformed churches, so their effect in inducing the capitalist spirit among their members was correspondingly weaker. Nevertheless, compared with Lutheranism outside pietistic circles, or Anglicanism outside Wesley's influence, their effect is significant, and accounts for the correlation between business success and Nonconformist religion, between Pietism and a reputation for skill and diligence as a worker.

Weber's thesis has given rise to continuous interest and criticism.

It has often been seen as principally opposed to a Marxist analysis because it allows more weight to the role of ideas in creating social structure than does Marxism. But in its immediate inspiration it refers more to Sombart's enquiry into the genesis of capitalism, published in 1902, than to any Marxist writing. Sombart argued for the predominant role of Jewry in the creation of Western European capitalism, and Weber, in rebutting this thesis, nevertheless looks for and finds a group, who in his own estimation rather resembled European Jewry, to fulfil the same catalytic role. In dealing with criticisms we should remember that Weber specifically argues that the role of religious belief was not to create capitalism out of nothing, but to combine with technical, political and other factors which were already favourable to such developments. We should also remember his general methodological standpoint that since all analyses of general historical problems are selective in their choice of material, no single one can be presented as the only correct answer.

Weber's earliest critics and commentators tended to take for granted the correlation between Reformed religion and the development of capitalism, but to question the argument that the second was the result of the first. Marxists argued that the Calvinist variety of Protestantism was an ideology used to justify free-market capitalism and the final rejection of the weakening controls of Catholic canon law on economic activities. Others argued that every advance in economic organisation and productivity was achieved by new men who had to break through entrenched practices and norms. The Calvinist entrepreneurs did no more and no less in this direction than the Catholic economic innovators, whether merchants, bankers or capitalist organisers of domestic artisans, of the medieval centuries. But as their economic breakthrough was achieved at a time when the unity of the church was, for different reasons, breaking up, their rebellion was expressed in religious terms also. Others again tried to show that the most important point both in Calvinism and capitalist development was the emphasis on individualism, or on a man's decisions according to his own conscience and his own view of his interests, regardless of the group, and this individualism was seen as a product, in both religious and economic contexts, of the Renaissance of the fifteenth century.

Later critics, in particular Samuelson,[3] have thrown doubt on the correlation between Calvinism and capitalism. Where it appears to hold, as in New England, or among the Huguenots, they find other reasons for the capitalist developments, and they add for good measure the cases where Calvinism took hold but was not coupled with speedy capitalist development, as in Scotland and Hungary. They also point to the cases where capitalism did develop but was not closely associated with Calvinist beliefs, as in England and Sweden. Even in the Netherlands, Samuelsson argues that detailed analysis of local religious and economic life suggests that the strictest Calvinism was found away from Amsterdam and other main centres of commercial development.

Although Weber believed that the Puritan, i.e., Calvinist, outlook stood at the cradle of modern economic man, he recognised that the child soon grew up and repudiated its nurse. The methodical ascetic activity of the first Calvinists was controlled by ministers just as anxious to bridle acquisitiveness as the canonists of medieval Christendom; but those who by successful entrepreneurship had grown wealthy tended either to leave Calvinistic religion (for example, the Methodist turning Anglican as he rose in social status), or to modify its tenets in a way which emphasised individualism and minimised social control of either getting or spending. This part of Weber's argument has been much more fully worked out by Tawney,[4] who traces the ways in which the nascent capitalism of medieval times, already escaping effective control by the Catholic Church, became the much stronger capitalism of the sixteenth and seventeenth centuries, in which religion's attempt to control the direction and pace of change became more and more unrealistic. As their ineffectiveness was realised, so political and ecclesiastical authorities and moralists began to rationalise their impotence and to develop theories of how, through the market, individual acquisitiveness resulted in collective benefit. On this view the power of Protestantism to encourage capitalism was, so far as it derived from asceticism, of short duration. What counted was the spur to individualism which the religion provided.

Tawney traces the kind of regulation of economic life which was attempted in the centuries just immediately before and after the Reformation, and shows how the scale and impersonality of capitalism made the application of ethical concepts extremely difficult. The same data can be examined to throw light on Weber's distinction between 'adventure capitalism' operating without ethical restraint, and 'rational capitalism' which he conceives as the methodical pursuit of profit coupled with asceticism in personal consumption. In the first, the capitalist accumulates wealth by luck, by piracy and by battening on political leaders in need of cash; having accumulated wealth he spends it lavishly, thus restricting his capacity to accumulate more by reinvestment. In the second, the capitalist gets rich by hard work, careful calculation of means to ends, readiness to innovate, and great frugality in expenditure. Thus he has more and more capital to reinvest. No doubt individuals could be found to correspond very exactly with those two types. But Weber's attribution of one type to pre-Reformation Catholic Europe, and of the other to Protestant Europe and New England, seems over-simple. In both cases the greatest opportunities to employ and accumulate capital lay in foreign trade, and in taking advantage of trading opportunities it is next to impossible to draw a dividing line between luck and hard work, between free individual enterprise and corporately privileged enterprise, especially in the war-torn circumstances of sixteenth- and seventeenth-century Europe. If the adventurer and the Puritan capitalist cannot be clearly distinguished in their mode of operation, neither can they in their use of profits. Some of the latter rivalled any Catholic prince in the lavishness of their expenditure.

In a sense, in spite of his misleading apparatus of two ideal types of capitalist radically opposed, Weber saw that in real life they tended to be confused. He accepts, as I have mentioned, that 'puritanical ideals tended to give way under excessive pressure from the temptation of wealth, as the Puritans themselves knew very well'.[5] Yet he clearly believes that at some stage the level of saving must be a crucial factor in the rise of capitalism, and that this level was raised by the influence of Calvinist asceticism. This factor of internal saving in capital formation has been much studied recently in more contemporary contexts, and no simple conclusion applicable to all cases seems possible. It is at least likely that the commercial development of Holland, England and New England, and of Huguenot cities in France, which seemed to Weber so striking, relied for its capital much more on the profits of trade and piracy than on the careful accumulation of the gains of hard work of hundreds of Calvinist artisans and petty traders. Conversely, the failure of Spain, Portugal and Catholic France to show the same rate of commercial development may be due to the disorders of warfare and the draining of free resources by taxation, as much as to the supposedly enervating consequences of the Catholic faith.

Tawney suggests that Weber, following Sombart, was stirred to study the social antecedents of capitalism by his experience of the current industrial revolution in Germany. It is interesting that, apart from his scanty and questionable data on occupational distribution and educational standards in relation to religion, he does not in fact seem to attach importance to the creative power of Protestantism in the German case.

In his study of the Protestant ethic and Calvinism Weber frequently uses two terms whose exact meaning requires some elucidation. The first is of his own coining—'inner-worldly asceticism'. The second is the general term 'rationalism' or 'rationalisation'. Both are also widely used in his comparative religious studies, and the second is a keyword in his whole sociology, so their meaning is of some importance.

In the context of Christianity Weber introduced the term 'inner-worldly asceticism' to contrast the Puritan activist with the Catholic monk. Both practised an ascetic way of life, the one in order to prove to himself his election to eternal life, the other in order to earn his salvation. In either case the religious belief inspired them to a way of life in which impulse was subordinated to a set pattern of activities, temptations to sensual indulgence were minimised, and self-discipline was exercised in such a way that all actions conduced to the attainment of the supreme goal of salvation. But whereas the monk saw his goal as necessitating a withdrawal from sexual and family life, from property and class relationships, and from political participation, the Calvinist believed that all these activities, if properly regulated and co-ordinated, could contribute to the fulfilment of God's will, and form part of that glorification of God on earth which was man's supreme duty. Weber saw the other-worldly asceticism of the monk as no more and no less demanding than the inner-worldly asceticism of the Puritan, and recognised that both were ideals capable of corruption in actual practice.

But he saw the results of each as different, since the closer the monk is to his ideal, the less influence, in Weber's view, can he have on the world; whereas the closer the Puritan is to his, the more influence he will have. Moreover, whereas the monk's way of life is a counsel of perfection for the few who have the vocation to it, the Puritan's strenuous self-discipline is commanded for all. Weber makes this contrast of other- and inner-worldly asceticism not only between Catholic religious and Calvinist man-of-affairs, but between Protestant Christianity on the one hand and Hinduism, Buddhism and Taoism on the other. The similarity to the Catholic position is most striking in the case of Buddhism, since this also is a religion encouraging monasticism and distinguishing between the full commitment of the monk and the half-way house of the lay believer. Weber is not disconcerted from calling Buddhist asceticism 'other-worldly' by discovering that Buddhist monasteries in China became large landowners, and in Tibet became the centres of political power, for these represent corruptions of the ideal, just as the involvement of Benedictines in medieval politics, or of Jesuits in post-Reformation politics, also represent corruptions of the ideal. He would argue that the initial precept of Buddhism, and its continuing *raison d'être*, is the depreciation of all actions designed to win worldly goals, from sexual satisfaction to wealth or political eminence. Therefore the tendency of Buddhism is always towards other-worldly asceticism, and therefore always away from any ethic which places a positive value on hard work and innovation in the economic field. Buddhism must always be a drag on economic development, particularly on those activities which require individual initiative and responsibility, for they tend to result in inequalities which contradict the brotherliness and detachment required by the religion.

Hinduism, which does not know the formal monasticism of the Buddhists, nevertheless has an analogous other-worldly asceticism in its philosophy and ethics. The ordinary activities of this world, familial, economic and political, are duties which must be carried out, but they are not the most important aspect of life. The great teachers show that the world of phenomena is a world of illusion. They show that by various means of physical self-discipline, meditation and prayer, men may perceive a reality beyond the transitoriness of material things and social relations. Beyond one's social and ritual duties lies the possibility of devoting oneself to these pursuits. The effort at understanding the world and mastering oneself lies always in the direction of other-worldly asceticism, and this, coupled with the strong magical elements in Hinduism and the divisive effects of caste, account in Weber's view for the obstacles to capitalist development which Indian society presents.

Finally in Taoism Weber discerns another religion which preaches asceticism, but not the inner-worldly variety thereof. The central tenet of Taoism is that there is a way or path of nature which man can also follow, provided that he limits self-seeking acquisitiveness, emulation and hostility. He does this best by withdrawing from activities which carry these temptations, rather than by valuing them as part of the way in which God's will can be fulfilled. Thus again contemplation, withdrawal from politics, subsistence rather than acquisition as an economic goal, follow from the Taoist position. This hindrance to capitalism, as is the case with Buddhism, is reinforced by the tendency to revert to magic and animism which Taoism, according to Weber, permits and even encourages.

If Buddhism, Taoism and Hinduism have all restricted economic development through their stress on other-worldly asceticism, and depreciation of activity in this world, other world religions have lacked the ascetic drive altogether, and therefore have in a different way also been unable to foster capitalism. Confucianism has continually emphasised a paternalistic kind of social structure in which individual inventiveness and enterprise were muted, and has thus restricted rather than encouraged change. Though it emphasises worldly values, the highest are those of benevolence and good faith, not the conquest of nature or the heroic achievement of an individual. Also, by its toleration of magic and animism, official Chinese religion has not cleared away obstacles to technical advance.

The position of Islam is different again, in Weber's view. He regards it as primarily a religion of warriors, oriented to worldly values of conquest and plunder. The warrior is fatalistic rather than methodical and self-disciplined, and asceticism of any kind is inappropriate. Weber admits that in some of the sufi brotherhoods of later Islam there are ascetic sects similar to those of lower-class Christian sects, but these have not been powerful enough to drive effectively towards economic development. Finally there is the case of Judaism, where Weber also discerns no high valuation of asceticism. Nevertheless, because of what Weber calls its 'pariah' position, and because it is to him a relatively rational religion, Judaism has from time to time played a significant part in economic advance and capitalist development. But lacking the ascetic values, it has only been able to develop the kind of political or adventure capitalism, which, as we have seen, Weber thought typical of the medieval period, and atypical of the capitalism of modern Europe and America.

These very broad generalisations must appear weakly based when presented in this very summary way. But even when backed up by Weber's encyclopaedic knowledge, doubts about them do arise. On Weber's own showing, capitalism cannot develop until a certain advance in trade, in division of labour, in money and banking, in maintenance of law and order and in the scope of the market has been achieved. His problem in fact is that these preconditions had been achieved in all civilisations, and yet only in the West did a capitalist society grow on these foundations. But if the other-worldiness of, say, Hinduism had not prevented the growth of large-scale kingdoms, of specialised crafts, of money and trade, law and administration, to roughly the same degree as these things had developed within Christendom, have we any grounds for saying that it nevertheless prevented subsequent advances in technique and economic organisation? Likewise, if the traditionalism of Confucianism had somehow accommodated itself to the developments of law, trade and techniques necessary to administer a vast regime, can we assume that somehow its adaptability thereafter failed, and it became a straitjacket against further development? Weber's comparisons of the economic advance of Europe since the sixteenth century with the relative stagnation or decline of Asiatic or Islamic societies requires to be carried out with much more attention to the factors other than religion which differentiate them one from another.

Without a great deal of further work it is impossible to regard Weber's conclusions as to the importance of the religious ethic in economic affairs as more than suggestive. But in emphasising the importance of attitudes and values, whether or not derived from religious teaching, he strikes, I think, a modern note. The great wealth of contemporary studies of underdeveloped countries and their problems show that development is not just a matter of quantities of capital and labour, and availability of technical knowledge, but that intangible factors of values and aspirations are also important.

I turn now to Weber's use of the terms 'rational' or 'rationalisation'. In *The Protestant Ethic and the Spirit of Capitalism* we are left to gather his meaning as we read, but in his subsequent essays, 'The Social Psychology of World Religions' and 'Religious Rejections of the World',[6] he discusses the terms quite fully. He has a further discussion in his *Theory of Social and Economic Organisation*, which was also written after the *Protestant Ethic*. From these works it is clear that he continued to be concerned with the problem of rationality, and that he found it necessary to make distinctions within this general term. In 'Social Psychology of World Religions', he says, 'we have to remind ourselves that rationalism may mean very different things. One thing is the kind of rationalisation the systematic thinker performs on the image of the world; an increasing theoretical mastery of reality by means of increasingly precise and abstract concepts. Rationalism means another thing if we think of the methodical attainment of a definitely given and practical end by means of increasingly precise calculation of adequate means. These types of rationalism are very different in spite of the fact that ultimately they belong inseparably together.'[7] Further on he writes, 'rationalism may also mean a systematic arrangement. In this sense the following methods are rational: methods of mortificatory or magical asceticism, of contemplation in its most consistent forms, e.g., in yoga, or in the manipulation of the prayer machines of later Buddhism. In general all kinds of practical ethics that are systematically and unambiguously oriented to fixed goals of salvation are rational, partly in the same sense as formal method is rational, and partly in the sense that they distinguish between "valid" norms and what is empirically given.'[8] This last quotation shows that Weber believes that 'rational' should not be equivalent to 'empirically grounded' or 'scientific', for the effectiveness of the means to salvation cannot be judged by empirical evidence. It also shows that he believed the word should be used from the point of view of the actor, and with reference to the actor's knowledge and conceptual categories. On this latter point I would judge that Weber, like most observers, finds it hard to be consistent. In most contexts, as we shall see, he calls magic and mysticism irrational, although from the actor's point of view their effectiveness in reaching the actor's goals may be as great as that of non-mystical types of religion. With regard to the rationality of the 'systematic thinker' and his 'theoretical mastery of reality', it is interesting to note that Weber holds the view that man cannot but strive to create intellectual systems which are internally consistent and link together all parts of his experience. Social conditions may foster or hinder this striving, and the actual construction and refinement of such systems is usually the prerogative of a group of specialists, priests and scholars. Yet the need for such a system is general, and therefore the creations of the specialists have some appeal to the masses. This is relevant to Weber's view, to be examined later, of the role of a priestly class in developing an ethical religion. It is also interesting to note that in his view there is an ultimate need for consistency between speculation or theorising on the one hand and experience on the other. This I take to be the meaning of the phrase that speculative and practical rationality 'ultimately belong inseparably together'.

Let us look at some of his examples of speculative rationality. He speaks of 'the rational need for a theodicy of suffering and dying',[9] and of the 'three rationally satisfying answers to the questioning of the basis of the incongruity between destiny and merit'.[10] Man's intelligence is bound to discover the problem of suffering and evil; it has also produced answers which, in Weber's view, are internally consistent, and give a consistent interpretation of all instances of suffering. These three 'rational' answers are, first, the Hindu doctrine of kharma, of a trans-migration of souls which through a cycle of existences compensates for injustice in any one life; second, Zoroastrian dualism, in which spiritual forces of good and evil are constantly ranged against one another, and injustice is a consequence of a temporary victory of evil spirits; and the 'predestination decree of the *deus abscondidus*',[11] i.e., the belief that God has such power and majesty that his acts are inscrutable to men, and cannot be judged by human standards. Any of these theories can make sense of all human experience, and none can be disproved by experience. Though entirely theoretical, they can, according to Weber, have important practical consequences. The first is bound to influence men towards resignation to suffering; the third may make for quietism and contemplation, but it may also, at least in its Christian Protestant forms, harp so much on men's guilt and inadequacy that it provokes them to ceaseless and disciplined activity in the service of God. The great creator God, who has preordained the whole of human history, may work in mysterious ways, yet history is nevertheless the working out of his purposes, and therefore action in this world is real and important. Thus the Judæo–Christian–Moslem conception of God as unfolding his purposes through history, tends to impel his followers to action, to moral effort and 'change for the better'. The Hindu–Buddhist conception of God or the divine, as withdrawn from phenomena, as an unchanging reality contrasted with a changing but not developing world of appearances, which underlies the doctrine of kharma, tends to encourage an unchanging social structure and a devaluation of activities which would upset it.

Weber's interpretations of these theoretical world-views are relevant to his studies of Christianity and capitalism, but I think he is more concerned in these studies with rationality in the practical sense, the 'increasingly precise calculation of adequate means for given and practical ends'. However, some difficulties in his usage do arise. One of the requirements for using the term in this sense is to be quite clear whether the judgement is made from the point of view of the actor, or the observer, who is supposedly better informed. Another is to be sure what the 'given ends' of the actors are, for if these cannot be known, the adequacy of means cannot be judged. This means that to impute greater or lesser rationality to actions of numbers of men is particularly difficult, for we know that it is characteristic of social action that unintended by-products always occur, not purposed by any of the participants. Therefore it is necessary to have independent evidence of goals and purposes; they cannot be inferred from the actions undertaken except in the simplest cases. The difficulty of imputing goals is compounded when the label 'rational' is applied to an ethical or legal or economic system, as Weber tends to do. Whose ends are in question when this is done? Is it implied that such a system meets the goals of all actors, or is there a covert switch from the meaning of 'rational' as instrumentally efficient, to the other meaning of 'systematic arrangement'? Finally there is the difficulty that if rational means efficiently purposive action, then its opposite, irrational, covers two different classes of action which need to be discriminated. There are, firstly, actions which are instrumental, which are done purely for the sake of a goal extrinsic to them, but where the means are inefficient. There are, secondly, actions which carry their own satisfaction, which are intrinsically worthwhile to the actors. For Weber, magic (*pace* the quotation given on p. 142) is usually deemed irrational, because its spells and medicines do not in fact achieve their goals of good health, victory, fertility, or any other 'practical end'. But, equally, he calls irrational artistic expression, erotic satisfactions, mystical raptures and states of ecstasy, although these are not means to an end but ends in themselves.

It is possible to trace the reason why Weber uses the word to cover these two different types of action by referring to his distinction, expounded in *Theory of Social and Economic Organisation*, between *zweckrational* and *wertrational* actions. The first he defines as action aimed at the achievement of a single limited goal, and the second as a pattern of actions all consistently directed to the achievement of a supreme value. In his discussions of religion and practical ethics, he uses the word 'rational' in the *wertrational* sense. Thus in Catholic Christian life he argues that only the monk is rational in that his life is lived under a rule in which each action contributes to the supreme goal. In Protestant Christianity only the Calvinist follows an equally methodical pattern of living. By emphasising what has to be given up in order to achieve this supreme goal, he implies that actions giving sensual satisfactions, e.g., of sex, cannot be part of a pattern of consistent purposes but must represent a diversion of energy on to disparate paths. That which is an end in itself cannot, in his view, also be a means to a goal. Intrinsically worthwhile actions are therefore called irrational. The Calvinist view that sexual activity, when directed to procreation, was good, was part of a rational ethic, because God had commanded men to multiply. On other terms, it made no contribution to the fulfilment of God's will and hence was irrational. The monastic view that God's service requires from some men that they should renounce sexual activity is equally rational. What, according to Weber, is not rational is an ethic which asserts that sexual enjoyment for its own sake is a goal which can be reconciled with other goals, and does not represent a purposeless and unwanted diversion of energy.

Accepting his own definition of *wertrational*, it seems that Weber is on even weaker ground in calling mystical states and artistic endeavour irrational, for there is surely strong evidence that these can be the controlling goal of human lives just as surely as Calvinist ethics or Catholic monastic rules. In fact it seems that the only controlling or supreme goal that Weber is able to accept is a goal beyond this world, spiritual salvation or eternal life. He frequently implies that the most rational life would be one in which all actions are purely instrumental, and are only undertaken by the actor in terms of his belief, well- or ill-founded, that they would help him to life eternal. Thus he deems Pietism less rational than Calvinism because it emphasises the value of spontaneous love and happiness here on earth, even though the Pietists, as much as the Calvinists, were concerned with the attainment of salvation beyond this world. In such usages rationalism tends to become equivalent to asceticism. This is confusing, because an ascetic renunciation is only rational if the actor, or the observer, is aware of the necessity to give up one thing in order to achieve another. Without knowing the range of ends of the actor it is impossible to judge whether his asceticism is rational or not. From his renunciation it is impossible to deduce his positive ends. In his treatment of *wertrationalität* in religious ethics, Weber seems to lose sight of his own warning that 'this simple proposition, which is often forgotten, should be placed at the beginning of every study which essays to deal with rationalism; it is possible to rationalise life from fundamentally different points of view in very different directions'.[12] It would have been easier to remember this warning if his terminology had enabled him to distinguish the irrational, in the sense of ineffective instrumental actions, from the non-rational, in the sense of intrinsically satisfying actions. In his categorisation of the four ideal types of social action, he includes 'affectual' action, but this is defined as blindly emotional in character, and thus is inappropriate to describe that vast range of actions which are expressive, but nevertheless purposive, which are ends in themselves but also means to further ends. In general, I would argue that his four pure types of social action—*zweckrational, wertrational*, affectual and traditional[13]—are all so extreme in formulation that they cannot be used as standards against which actual patterns of action can usefully be compared. Neither is it useful to construct mixed types on a purely quantitative basis of how much rationality, emotion or traditionalism is involved. The actual content of attitudes, feelings and doctrines needs also to be brought in to the construction of a typology of purposiveness or rationality.

This point is particularly relevant to Weber's comparative analysis of different systems of religious ethics. The supreme value of the Calvinist was 'to glorify God', but this is an entirely empty phrase unless we know that he believed that this meant the fulfilment of the biblical commandments in both the Old and New Testaments. It is given a still more precise content when we know that the Calvinists believed that they had biblical warrant for a particular non-episcopal form of church government, and for a particular interpretation of the doctrines of God's omnipotence and man's sinfulness. Even so, there was plenty of room for disagreement between sects and individuals as to the best way of carrying out these beliefs in practice. Did they require a church whose discipline would cover the rebellious and apathetic? Or would God be better glorified by a gathering of the saints into conventicles apart from sinners? Would the goal best be served by fighting Catholic monarchs as well as Catholic principles, or by withdrawing from political entanglements and setting up new communities? All these questions received differing answers, and the acceptance of the same supreme value— 'to glorify God'—did not entail the acceptance of the same path of day-to-day conduct. This simple phrase did not do away with great complications in the relations of means to ends, nor with the possibility that for the Calvinist, as for any other kind of Christian, self-interest, love of power and wealth would enter into his calculations of means towards the supreme goal. In terms of overall patterns of living, Weber seems to give the Calvinist too high a score in relation to the ideal of *wertrationalität*, and all other kinds of Christian too low a one. In particular, he does not recognise that emulative striving for power and wealth, which some Calvinists certainly thought compatible with their religion, may introduce as much 'non-rationality', if not actual 'irrationality', into a religious ethic, as sexual and sensual indulgence.

There is yet one further point to be made about Weber's use of rationality in relation to systems of ethics and economic life. He states, 'it is above all the impersonal and economically rationalised (but for this very reason ethically irrational) character of commercial relationships that evokes the suspicion of ethical religion'.[14] Obviously, there are here two opposite meanings of rational, according to the qualification, economic or ethical; what is economically rational is ethically irrational. Yet in the *Protestant Ethic* he has constantly referred to the 'rational economic ethic' of Calvinism. The clue to this apparent confusion lies in his very useful distinction between 'formal' and 'substantive' rationality of economic action. The former he defines as 'the extent of quantitative calculation or accounting which is technically possible or actually applied'. Substantive rationality is 'the degree to which a given group of persons is or could be adequately supplied with goods by means of an economically oriented course of social action. This course of action will be interpreted in terms of a given set of ultimate values no matter what they may be. In principle, there is an indefinite number of possible standards of value which are rational in this sense.'[15] It is clear, I think, that in all his comparative studies of religion, Weber is thinking of formal rationality, and arguing that a free-enterprise market economy is formally the most rational, in that for every individual placed therein, it gives the greatest possibility of 'quantitative calculation or accounting' of man's efforts and satisfactions. Most satisfactions are obtainable through the market, efforts and satisfactions have prices measured in the same money units, and these prices are the same for everyone. Just as the market operates impartially between persons, so it generates and relies upon a legal system which operates impartially and is no respecter of persons. In such a system, both politically and economically, arbitrariness and partiality are reduced to a minimum. And though relative riches and poverty persist, the system is increasingly rational in that it produces a continuous improvement of techniques and organisation, according to the intensity of needs revealed in relative prices. Thus production of goods and services continuously increases, and those human needs which can be satisfied through the market are satisfied at a higher level. Yet the substantive rationality of the system is a separate problem. There are values not realisable through the market, such as equality, cooperation, local loyalty or national glory, and whether a market system fosters or destroys them is an open question. Weber himself was inclined, according to his own set of values, to see losses in substantive rationality due to those processes of industrialisation which represented a marked advance in formal rationality. As all ethical religions emphasise the importance of brotherly or parental-filial relations among members, a market economy cannot but be substantively irrational to them. This part of Weber's analysis needs to be remembered; otherwise it is only too easy to read him as an apologist for capitalism on grounds of its greater rationality.

It remains to deal with two other important aspects of Weber's treatment of religion in complex societies; his contrast of priestly and prophetic religion, and his correlation of particular religions with the social groups (for example, scholars and artisans) which effectively carried them. Weber sees the differentiated roles of priest and magician as one of the first and most universal forms of the division of labour in society. In preliterate peoples, the family heads and chiefs may carry out all rituals, and magical and mythical knowledge may be available on equal terms to all. Yet even among these peoples there is often some degree of specialisation. The chief may be helped by ritual specialists; magical knowledge and power may be acquired by a process of initiation and apprenticeship which only a few undergo. Weber draws the division between magic and religion along the line of coercion or entreaty of spirits or supernatural forces. The priest, as a specialist in entreating the gods by prayer and sacrifice, is usually differentiated further from the magician in terms of his corporate organisation, formal selection and training. 'The crucial feature of the priesthood is the speciali- sation of a particular group of persons in the continuous operation of a cultic enterprise, permanently associated with the particular norms, places and times, related to specific social groups.'[15] (This is clearly a wider definition than that implied in the Christian distinctions between priest and minister. It is intended to include Moslem mullahs and imams, Protestant ministers and Jewish rabbis, as well as priests who have a special sacramental role.) Though Weber points to occasional cases of guilds and brotherhoods of magicians, he believes that most frequently magicians work as individuals whose services are solicited by individuals or groups as the need arises. Their organisation is accidental, not necessary as in the case of priests because of the continuous or regular operation of a cult. He also declares that magicians generally derive their position from personal charismatic qualities, inherited or acquired through personal experience of ordeals or other kinds of initiation. Though social norms may prescribe the qualities necessary for an effective magician, and the kind of training which creates and develops them, the individual must prove his possession of these qualities; his power is in himself, not his office. The priest on the other hand is recognised as such when he has mastered the doctrine and ritual of the cult; he does not require special qualities of temper- ament, nor does he constantly have to prove himself by success and in competition with others.

Weber stresses the mutual development of priesthood and doctrine in the religions of civilised societies. 'The full development of both a metaphysical rationalisation and a religious ethic requires an independent and professionally trained priesthood, permanently occupied with the cult or with the practical problems involved in the care of souls'.[17] This is partly a matter of granting to some the leisure needed for such theorising, since Weber thinks that there is an innate human drive to find meaning in life which will produce metaphysical and ethical results when not submerged by immediate practical needs. Where, as in imperial China, priestly functions were carried out by the emperor and his administrators, not by full-time priests, there was a development of ethics and political theory, but not of metaphysical religion. Somewhat similarly, in the Graeco–Roman world, priestly functions were either part of domestic and political roles, or fragmented among a number of priestly colleges serving quite different cults. As a consequence, there was no great growth of philosophy and ethics among priests; it was a different class of philosophic teachers who gave rein to the drive to speculate or systematise. But even in these cases, and still more obviously where a fully professional priesthood developed, Weber argues that with the growth of each civilisation there developed a belief in a single divine order which gave moral significance to human life. The gods ceased to be amoral and discrete forces, and came to be viewed as creators or sustainers of a cosmic moral order. Weber attributes this development to the larger scale of political and social order, and the need for deliberate legislative activity to create and maintain it, together with a growing understanding of, and reliance on, the regularities of nature. The impact of these social changes on the priestly and scholarly class gave rise to monotheistic or pantheistic thought. The priesthood were 'the bearers of the systematisation and rationalisation of religious ethics'.[18] In that task the priests were in conflict with the magicians, or, rather, the rationalisation of religious ethics was continually hampered by the prevalence of magical attitudes. Weber, rather like J. G. Frazer, sees rationalised religion as a thin crust of belief overlaying a continual predisposition by the masses to magical explanations and manipulations of events. It is therefore always possible that the doctrine and ritual developed by a priesthood will be invaded and corrupted by magical notions. A tension between the educated priests and the people pressed hard by material necessities always exists, and though the experience of large-scale social order, and the growing knowledge of the laws of nature, promotes a rational religious interpretation of the world, this interpretation is always at risk from magic.

It may also be at risk because each priestly doctrine tends to justify and sanctify a particular social order, and if this order is destroyed the credibility of their system weakens. A dramatic case of this is the practical extinction of Zoroastrian religion with the political conquest of the Persian Empire. Japanese Shintoism suffered extensive revision after the defeat in 1945 of the imperial system with which it was linked. Priestly religion, once it has developed to the point of monotheism or pantheism, is socially conservative, and its fortunes are linked with particular social orders. But a traditional order may be challenged from within as well as from without, particularly when its scale and complexity are such as to produce great diversities of wealth and political power. These challenges are led by prophets, who rival the priests as 'bearers of the systematisation and rationalisation of religious ethics'. The prophet is like the priest in the rationalising task he performs, but like the magician in being called to it on the basis of personal charismatic qualities. 'The priest lays claim to authority by virtue of his service in a sacred tradition, whilst the prophets' claim is based on personal revelation and charisma.'[19] Weber grants that many prophets, proclaiming new or renewed religion, have also been magicians, particularly since they have justified their claim to a hearing by magical practices of divination and healing. But the essence of their mission is religious and ethical. Thus Buddha preached a new doctrine of man's nature which undermined the ethics of caste and provided a foundation for a new kind of group, the order of mendicant monks. The Hebrew prophets gave a new view of what God required of men: not sacrifice, but brotherly conduct and social justice. They thereby provided an essential basis for the continuation of Hebrew society through the period of political disaster and exile. Christ in his turn proclaimed a universal law of love and a new doctrine of God's redemptive relationship with his world. He initiated a new social organisation—the church—within the old one. Mohammed proclaimed an uncompromising monotheism which carried within it the ethical obligation of unity among the warring tribes and clans, and so built up the new community of the faithful.

The priest is the servant of an existing order, the prophet is the centre of a new one. The priest typically receives regular fees or maintenance; the prophet depends on gifts and alms, for his new message is of criticism or even rebellion against the established order, from which he must assert his independence. To the degree that he is successful he must attract and organise a new community. Thus prophecy lies at the beginning of congregational religion.

To Weber one of the sociologically important features of prophecy is that it can wrench the masses away from magic and superstition more radically than traditional priestly religions. These, as we have seen, attempt to teach a more systematic metaphysic or morality, but their impact is lessened either because their views are too subtle and complex to be grasped by ordinary folk, or because their ethical idealism seems to be distorted in favour of justifying a status quo which to many seems unjust. Also, since groups of priests have vested interests in particular cults, their drive to synthesise in a monotheistic direction may be weakened by their interest in perpetuating a particular cult. Thus the lesson taught to the masses is not clearly monotheistic, and magical ideas find an easy entrance. This, to Weber, is particularly true of Hinduism and Buddhism.

Prophets, according to Weber, can only arise in large-scale literate civilisations, where thought has already reached beyond the magical or mythical, and where social structure is sufficiently complex for some groups to be potentially critical or rebellious. A leader who can convince himself and others that he has divine authority for a new form of society can then get a hearing. But Weber is prepared to go further than this in suggesting how prophecy is linked with particular forms of society. He first distinguishes emissary from exemplary prophets; the first is seen as an emissary of God with a message to preach to mankind; the second as a vessel of God, who by the example of his God-directed life leads others to imitate him. Thus Moses and the Hebrew prophets, Zoroaster, Mohammed and Jesus are to Weber emissary prophets; whilst Buddha is the supreme example of the exemplary prophet. He asserts that emissary prophets have only been known in Western and Near Eastern societies, whilst exemplary prophets typically arise in Far Eastern civilisations, and he connects this with the fact that the Near Eastern societies have a clearer conception of the transcendence of God than do those of India, China and Japan. This conception of the transcendent supramundane God he holds to have arisen in reflection of the supreme political power of the emperor in Persia, Egypt, Imperial Rome, etc., against the lesser personal authority of the head of state in India, China and other Far Eastern societies. This generalisation about correspondence between political order and theological concepts is very Durkheimian in character. It is, however, but weakly supported by the evidence, for the clearest case of a transcendent monotheism is that of the Hebrews, whose kingship was relatively weak and temporary. Weber himself argues that the Hebrews arrived at their conception of God not through direct experience of an absolute monarchy of their own, but rather through observation of their neighbours! Why then did these neighbours fail to develop an even clearer notion of a supramundane God?

It also goes against Weber's generalisation that many examples of prophetic movements can be found among primitive peoples brought into sudden and disturbing contact with more powerful civilisations. Yet the traditional religion that they alter may have been but faintly monotheistic, and the traditional society not at all despotic, or priest-ridden.

Nevertheless Weber's speculations about the social causes of prophetic movements throw into relief the interesting question of whether great prophets should be looked on as so many sociological 'sports', or whether their appearance is correlated with specific social structures or processes. It also highlights the occasions which appear to falsify Durkheim's generalisation that a religious system expresses and reinforces an existing pattern of society.

Weber's theory of the social origins and consequences of prophetic religion cannot be fully assessed without some consideration of his concept of charisma. This word, which he takes from the Greek, is translated in Christian writings as 'grace'. But Weber uses it in a much wider sense in his general sociology as part of his classification of types of authority. The three ideal types of authority he postulates are charismatic, traditional and rational-legal. All empirically occurring cases can be considered as approximations to, or mixtures of, these three types. When authority is traditional, obedience is given to long-standing customary rules, and to men holding traditional positions of leadership in which their first duty is to maintain these rules. In the rational-legal case, obedience is given to a system of law, and to men holding official positions, whose power derives from and is circumscribed by law. But in the case of charismatic authority, obedience is given to a leader accepted for his 'exemplary personal qualities'. Charismatic authority is therefore always novel, not springing from an existing social structure of differential statuses and roles. From whatever group in society he comes, he emerges as a person trusted and followed for his personal qualities, not as the representative of a pre-existing group, or as the occupant of an office. Those qualities may be of military talent, political leadership, religious prophecy, or cultural innovation; it is through them that he gathers a following. However, this following, once gathered, has to be organised; rules will be made and customs established, and, as the life of the group goes on, the pattern of authority will become more rational-legal or traditional in character. By definition, charismatic authority can appear as a pure type only transiently, during the period when the leader emerges and collects his disciples. At the death of the leader, further changes must occur. The group may disperse altogether, as it may also do before the leader's death if his luck fails and success does not confirm his possession of special talents. But if the group does continue, there will be, according to Weber, some belief among the members either in hereditary charisma or the charisma of office. The conception of personal qualities is here undergoing transformation into a conception of a transmissible, though immaterial power, which could light on the most ordinary personality and give it authority. An example of hereditary charisma is the choice of the first caliphs of Islam from among the descendants of the prophet; an example of charisma of office is the development of the papacy in Western Christendom. These aspects of 'routinisation of charisma', as the time of the original prophecy recedes, suggest that Weber had in mind some special differentiating quality of religious organisation, whose pattern of authority cannot be described simply in terms of the gradual expansion of traditional or rational-legal elements at the expense of the charismatic. If the prophet succeeds not only in establishing a transient congregation but a long-lasting church or sect, then his successors will be, in Weberian terminology, priests rather than prophets. But, as priests, they derive their authority from a relation to a cult and the god that it serves, and are never quite assimilated to secular authority, although the degree of their separateness may vary. It therefore appears that Weber's prophets do not represent merely the religious variety of the species, charismatic authority, but a rather special sub-group, in that religious innovators have shown themselves capable, in favourable circumstances, of originating new groups whose basis is to some extent different from secular authority, and whose boundaries, in most cases, are much wider than those of any secular authority.

I would emphasise that Weber's concept of charismatic authority is properly sociological—it is not just the 'great man' view of history dressed up in new words, for he recognises that the special personal qualities of the new leader must find a response, and that some groups will respond to one set of qualities and some to another. He stresses the frequency with which prophets lay claim to the capacity to work miracles, or have such abilities attributed by their followers to them, but this only shows how widespread and general is the need to believe in magic. Other qualities in the leader may evoke a more limited response, and Weber tries to identify the groups which have responded first to the great religious prophets. In the case of the Hebrew prophets, he believes that this was the peasant and artisan class, who responded to the prophecy that only through brotherliness and social justice could the people escape political disaster. In the case of Mohammed it was the urban poor who resented the rule, and the internecine strife, of the wealthy clan-based oligarchies, and therefore welcomed the message of the equality of all under a supreme God. In the case of Buddha, the appeal was to those members of an educated upper class who disliked the powers of an established priesthood which battened on the superstitions of the masses and sanctioned the social divisiveness of caste. In the case of Jesus, the first recognition of his message beyond the limits of Jewry was by town-dwellers, who by migration had lost touch with the old communal religions, and by social position tended to be critical of, or at least unconcerned with, political power and wealth. Weber's discussion of prophecy thus leads on to his argument that for each of the great religions there is a particular class or group acting as its 'bearer', marking it with its particular needs and aptitudes. For him, Confucianism, Brahminic Hinduism and early Buddhism are *par excellence* the religions of *literati*, of a group skilled in dialectic and conceptual thinking, and living at one remove from the pressing necessity of gaining their daily bread. Primitive Christianity bears the impress of the values of the urban masses, their need for mutual charity in new communities. As artisans rather than peasants, they were more easily weaned away from magic towards an ethical religion, but the ethics that appealed to them were the ethics of the small group, remote from political problems, and they welcomed a doctrine of personal rather than collective salvation. Islam, though its first followers were somewhat similar, was easily adapted to the needs of warriors, since Mohammed and his followers found themselves in the position of conquerors on a vast scale.

This question of the mutual influence between a new religious prophecy, and those attracted by it, clearly is a very important one, but also very complex. Wide though Weber's knowledge of the history of religions was, his treatment of each of the great religions is cursory compared with his detailed analysis of Calvinism and the capitalist class in *The Protestant Ethic*. By the standard which he there set himself, his other works on Confucianism, Hinduism and Buddhism are suggestive rather than authoritative. Clearly some religions have spread among socially very disparate groups. Christianity may have appealed only to the urban artisans in its first century of existence; in the second and subsequent centuries it appealed to all classes, and to rural as well as urban populations. Islam may have been borne, in quick succession, by the urban poor, and by the successful armies into which they were transformed; it has since become the religion of as many varieties of men and groups as Christianity. Buddhism likewise has spread to a variety of peoples. Clearly the fit between one group's needs and a religious prophecy need not be such as to prevent successful proselytisation among other groups. Equally clearly the successive groups of converts alter the prophetic message to a closer accord with their needs and traditions. But not all prophecies have expanded their audience in size and variety. Zoroastrianism and post-prophetic Judaism have become in the course of their history religions borne by a much narrower range of groups, entirely urban and non-military, and largely commercial. How much of the original message persists in these circumstances? Are there any limits to the possible changes in theology and ethics within a given religious tradition? Weber contents himself with saying that the original message always retains some influence, and this is tantamount to saying that the first group to take it up is more influential than any others to which it spreads.

Weber's view that each religion has its own 'bearer', and each broad type of human group its own particular religious need and aptitude, has some Durkheimian flavour. But it is clear that with regard to prophetic religion, and to a lesser extent even with regard to priestly religion, Weber attributes to religious factors a more creative, and less merely reflective, role than Durkheim.

Some commentators have interpreted Weber as predicting the onset of a totally secular and irreligious society, but his views do not all lend support to this thesis. His famous phrase for our contemporary Western situation, *die Entzaüberung des Weltes*, which is always translated as 'the disenchantment of the world', refers to the final disappearance of magical ideas, not religious ones. His insistence that men necessarily strive for an all-embracing and consistent interpretation of the world is compatible with their retention or abandonment of religion, unless the meaning of religion is so stretched as to include any world-view. Weber is clearly not in sympathy with such an extension of its meaning, as can be seen from his refusal to accord Confucian ethics full religious status. As I understand it, he thinks of this striving as an intellectual effort, and does not think that its products will necessarily have the function of comforting men in distressful situations, as modern functionalist writers seem often to imply for religious systems of thought. Nor does he consider the possible uses of ritual in social life, beyond the intellectually primitive stages of magical casting of spells, or sacrifice on the *do ut des* principle.

It is true that he traces in the economics, politics and science of the modern world the growth of both rationality and secularism, but 'rationality' here is clearly meant in the *zweckrational* sense, the increasingly efficient adaption of means to particular limited ends. But I repeat that he also regards the striving for a comprehensive world-view as an essential and persisting theme of human life, and it is not clear that a world-view which gives weight to moral and aesthetic experience is necessarily going to be irreligious. In the more fundamental sense of rationality, i.e., substantive rationality of social life, or *wertrationalität* of personal life, it is an open question whether, according to Weber's scheme of thought, growth in rationality is in conflict with theistic religion. Neither is it clear that Weber would correlate the present degree of secularisation with an increase of rationality in this more profound sense.

1. M. Weber, *The Protestant Ethic and the Spirit of Capitalism*, 1904.

2. ibid., p. 58.

3. K. Samuelsson, *Religion and Economic Action*, 1961.

4. R. H. Tawney, *Religion and the Rise of Capitalism*, 1927.

5. M. Weber, op. cit., p. 174.

6. 'Religious Rejections of the World and their Directions' and 'Social Psychology of the World Religions', in *Essays from Max Weber*, trans. by H. Gerth and C. W. Mills, 1947.

7. ibid., pp. 293–4.

8. ibid., pp. 293–4.

9. ibid., p. 275.

10. ibid., p. 275.

11. ibid., p. 275.

12. M. Weber, *The Protestant Ethic and the Spirit of Capitalism*, p. 77.

13. M. Weber, *Theory of Social and Economic Organisation*, trans. by T. Parsons and A. Henderson, 1947, pp. 104–7.

14. M. Weber, *Sociology of Religion*, trans. by E. Fischoff, 1966.

15. M. Weber, *Theory of Social and Economic Organisation*, p. 170.

16. M. Weber, *Sociology of Religion*, p. 30.

17. ibid., p. 30.

18. ibid., p. 45.

19. ibid., p. 46.

8

RELIGION IN INDUSTRIAL SOCIETIES

The discussion of church, sect and denomination in Chapter 5 necessarily trespassed on the question of the influence of industrialisation on religion; we noted that in contemporary industrial societies sects exist, but not in great numerical strength. But industrialisation has had its impact on aspects of religious belief and practice other than the incidence of sectarianism, and it is to these broader questions that I now turn.

Industry and urbanism are currently affecting the lives of millions outside the established industrial societies of Western Europe and America, and a full consideration of the issues should cover these industrialising societies too. However, lack of space and limited information forbid this, so that apart from a few preliminary remarks about other countries I shall deal only with the position in Western Europe and the USA. There is one advantage in this, because these societies show not only the effects of rapid transition towards a predominantly industrial society, but of the later stage of settled town life and a much higher standard of living.

The most industrialised country outside those of the Judæo–Christian tradition is undoubtedly Japan. For many centuries Japan has been a society of two religions, Shinto and Buddhism, each very different from the other. Shinto is essentially a ritual protection of the community, local and national, by the worship of deities associated with earth, sun, moon and other natural forces. The most important of these were, until 1945, connected with the religious sanctity of the Emperor, but there were many others in which local deities were worshipped at local shrines. Membership in the local community was tantamount to membership of the group worshipping at the local shrine. Buddhist temples, however, had a following arising from kinship ties rather than neighbourhood ties, and the main function of the Buddhist temple was to conduct funeral rites and the connected celebration of the ancestors. As the functions of Shinto shrine and Buddhist temple were distinct, most Japanese adhered to both systems, though occasionally a Buddhist group would proclaim a more exclusive doctrine.

Migration to the towns upset both the village-based Shinto cults and the kin-based Buddhist congregations. The period of modernisation beginning in 1862 saw a deliberate attempt by the government to elaborate a national Shinto cult which could be practised throughout the land, but this effort met with little success. On the other hand, forms of sectarian Shinto, which had begun in an earlier period, grew rapidly in popularity in the 1880s and 1890s. These sects were formed, independently of local ties, from the followers of a charismatic leader. They stressed traditional values of family duty and service to the state, but demanded more of their members, ritually and ethically, than the traditional Shinto or Buddhism of the period. They are believed to have recruited mostly from among the lower classes. Some of these sects have followed the path to denominational status, and taken their place among the 153 different Shinto organisations recognised today.

After the defeat of 1945, and the further spurt of industrial development, there appeared some new forms of Buddhism generally characterised as sects. The new groups recruit largely in the cities, to which the older religious forms have not been successfully transplanted. A Japanese writer has suggested that their intense ritual and social life has a particular appeal to those who have moved to the towns but have not found employment in the large paternalistic firms which provide both status and security to their employees. The largest of the sects, Soka Gakkai, claims a membership of about 4% of the population.

The extent of religious belief and practice in modern Japan is very difficult to estimate statistically. An opinion survey held in 1961 reported that only 35% of the adult population had a religious faith, which suggests that industrialisation has had a widespread secularising influence. Yet census statistics show 148 million memberships in religious groups in a population of approximately 100 million.[1] It seems that as far as census returns are concerned, the pattern of double adherence to Shinto and Buddhism persists in about half the population, but apparently this adherence is conceived by very large numbers to have no significance as an acceptance of a religious faith. This is the reverse of the position in Britain today, where far more people give affirmative answers to questions about their religious faith than are practising members of any religious group.

Overall we may surmise that the changes in Japanese religion in the past century of industrialisation have been towards a large-scale abandonment of old rituals and beliefs and a smaller-scale eruption of powerful devotion to new sectarian variants of the old religions. Similar phenomena, as we shall see, have occurred in other industrialising countries. However, though the new offshoots of Shinto and Buddhism may rightly be called sects in that they make quite untraditional demands on their members in respect of ritual and organisation, the moral values they proclaim are traditional—the unity of the nation, family piety and public service. They show none of the qualities, underlined by Troeltsch and others, of antagonism to the social order and emphasis on the virtues of humility and other-worldliness. It must be remembered, in analysing the Japanese version of sectarianism, that industrialisation has been accompanied by tremendous political vicissitudes; the nationalistic character of the new groups may be a response to these rather than to the new kind of economy.

In one respect the Japanese experience is being repeated in other industrialising societies. It is clear that any cult which is tied closely to kin groups or locality will lose support when many people move away from their kin and native village. This does not necessarily imply the loss of all religious practice, since new cults may spring up in the towns, or there may be more conversions to proselytising religions such as Islam or Christianity. In some of the growing towns of sub-Saharan Africa, it seems that the townsman's faith shows features of both innovation and conversion. For example, the urban Bantu are Christian, but their churches are very often single congregations formed around a popular leader, who may innovate doctrine or ritual without reference to any outside ecclesiastical organisation. Such groups may be sectarian only in the sense of cutting themselves off from established churches or denominations, or they may be sectarian also in their opposition in Christian terms to European domination in religious, political and economic matters. Yet in spite of the popularity of African congregational Christianity, and of Islam, it seems probable that in the new urban and industrial populations more people are left out of any system of religious practice than in the traditional rural society, where participation in such practice was simply part of belonging to the community.

Other societies in which current processes of industrialisation are undoubtedly having an effect on religion are the Communist countries of Europe and Asia, where the old faiths are officially discouraged and sometimes actively persecuted. The difficulty is to distinguish the effects of repression and discouragement from those of urbanisation and industry. That the latter have had some independent effect may be deduced from the changes in religious practice and affiliation which occurred after freedom of worship was granted in Russia in 1905. Immediately it became apparent that loyalty to the church had declined much more in the growing towns than in the countryside. This urban-rural differential has persisted to the present day. In some of the new towns of Eastern Russia and Siberia there seems to be hardly any organised religious life; a town of 500,000 inhabitants may have but one church. But political repression may stimulate as well as discourage religious life and some observers claim a significant increase in the membership of both old and new sects in Communist Russia.

In all Communist countries the ruling ideology is clothed in ritual forms such as parades, collective chanting of slogans, pilgrimages to the mausoleum of Lenin. If these are to be considered functionally equivalent to the religious rituals of the old faiths, it would be very interesting to know whether their appeal to the population is greater where the old rituals have practically vanished, as in the big new towns, or in more traditional settings. Does an uprooted population crave for new symbols to replace the old ones which have lost their meaning, or do such populations manage well enough without any collective rituals? (Of course, in the communist case, the new rituals are organised by the bureaucracy; the question is whether they have a meaning and a strong appeal to the people at large.) Answers to this question would throw some light on the functional theory of religion in modern society, which tends to adopt the position that religion in one form or another is essential to society. It is tantalising that information from these societies is so scanty and hard to evaluate.

On the position of religion in industrialised Europe and America information is more plentiful. Let us see whether it enables us to answer questions on the effect of industrialisation on traditional and new religions, and on the possibility of a differential effect on Catholic, Protestant and Jewish populations.

About the impact of industrialisation there is relevant historical as well as contemporary data. One of the most important pieces of evidence in respect of Britain is the 1851 religious census. This effort to measure the proportion of the population attending a place of worship on a normal Sunday was made after a century of rapid industrialisation, in the course of which many warning voices about the weakness of the churches in the new industrial towns had been heard. The result of the census bore out these warnings. Although over the country as a whole nearly one in two of the population had attended church, in the big towns it was nearer to one in three. In the rural areas the figure was about two in three. But despite the broad inverse correlation between size of town and level of church attendance, there were exceptions, which suggested that the process of industrialisation was not a simple direct cause of irreligion, or at least of lack of religious practice. First, there was the low rate of attendance in London, which was not then an industrial town in the sense of having numerous large factories. Its population had grown as rapidly as that of the factory and mining areas, but Londoners' occupations were largely in services, distribution and small-scale industries. Yet its church-going figures were as low as those of Manchester, Sheffield and Birmingham. Moreover, its reputation for lack of religious practice ante-dated such industrialisation as it had experienced. This suggested that life in large towns, regardless of whether they were predominantly industrial, tended to weaken religious practice. On the other hand, the 1851 figures revealed that some large towns had higher than average church attendances; these were towns that had not been revolutionised by large-scale industry, but had grown by extending their old functions of marketing, professional and administrative services. They had grown with the population, but their expansion had been more gradual than that of London or the big factory and port towns. This implied that it is not so much the large scale of town life as the rate at which this large scale is reached, that is associated with a decline in church-going. Industrialisation is not a single and simple process, and the effects of each different component on religious practice needs to be traced. In this respect the 1851 census suggests further questions rather than providing all the answers. Another aspect of industrialisation in the nineteenth century was the growth of a working class with its own organisations, such as cooperatives, unions and friendly societies. The census could not directly measure class differentials in church-going, but its figures are quite consonant with the widely held impression that the working class was more indifferent to religion than the middle classes. Nevertheless, remembering that by usual definitions the working class comprised at least 80% of the population the census showed that even in the big towns with the lowest attendance rates at least one in eight of the working class attended church. Over the whole country, the proportion was perhaps as high as one in three.[2]

But it was Nonconformity, not the Church of England, which gathered the largest number of working-class adherents. The Baptists' revival, which brought them a fourfold increase in members in the first half of the nineteenth century, began in the working class, though it made most progress in the smaller rather than in the larger industrial areas, and in some parts of rural England. The various branches of Methodism increased fivefold in the same period, and were able to unite regional and religious sentiment in Wales and Cornwall. The successive schisms in Methodism showed that it attracted large numbers of working-class followers, for it was tension between these and the middle-class leadership which provoked the splits. The largest of these seceding groups was the Primitive Methodists, whose membership of around 100,000 in 1851 compared with 300,000 Wesleyan Methodists. The ratio of these two figures suggests the ratio of working to middle class in Methodism generally. The Primitives, who used highly emotional revivalist meetings to bring in converts, had their successes among rural as well as industrial proletarians. For instance, in Norfolk, where the 'closed' villages under the domination of a single landowner remained firmly Anglican, the 'open' villages of poor cottagers and squatters were a fertile field for Primitive Methodist evangelists.

The 1851 census gives us insight into the effects of industrialisation on religious practice, because at that date there was great variation in the degree of change caused by industrialisation in different parts of the country, therefore, comparisons between different areas throw light on the question. But a direct comparison over time is much more difficult, since nothing like the 1851 census was attempted before or since. Studies of parishes in pre-industrial England are few and far between. Such as they are, they suggest great differences in church attendance, with possibly the leadership and discipline of the squire and landlord as an important factor. If he were lax, or an absentee from the village, his tenants and dependents might be lax too. A recent study[3] of some local Catholic congregations in eighteenth-century England distinguishes between 'seigneurial' and 'independent' congregations, and finds religious practice higher in the first type. A similar division might throw light on variations of Anglican practice also. The widespread failure to attend church in the new towns could then be seen as an escape from dependency rather than the deliberate repudiation of a set of beliefs and practices. For there was not a great growth of secularism—though the Chartists did chant 'more pigs, less parsons'—and baptism, religious marriage and burial continued to be practically universal practices. We have seen, in charting the rise of Methodism and the Baptists, that the escape from dependency could be, for a sizable fraction of the working class, an entrance into new forms of religious organisation in which the laity played an important role, and democratic principles were in some degree applied.

Measurements of working-class involvement with Noncomformity do not distinguish the various levels or types within the mass of wage-earners. But all impressions agree that it was the skilled and regularly employed men and their families who were most likely to join or attend the chapels. William Booth left the Methodists to found the Salvation Army because he found the former were unable to appeal effectively to the mass of unskilled workers. The Primitive Methodist membership in the second half of the nineteenth century rose and fell in rhythm with economic boom and slump, suggesting that prosperity encouraged membership. On the other hand, the second half of the nineteenth century, when the worst hardships of industrialisation were over, and more workers were attaining a standard of living above bare subsistence, did not see such a spectacular advance in Nonconformity as the first half. Numbers advanced only a little faster than total population. By this time, there was some loss of richer members who drifted back to the Church of England, but this was probably not numerically important. The slower advance of Nonconformity during the heyday of Victorian 'progress', and its limitation and decline in the twentieth century, suggest that in Britain, at least, the effect of the second century of industrialisation is to increase religious indifference, not only among the very poor, but at all levels of society. This is borne out by the trends of confirmation and active practice in the Anglican Church during the same period. Whether the intervening variables are urbanisation, affluence, occupational changes, education, or some other unsuspected factor, is far from clear. But it does seem that some different combination of causes is at work than the social disorganisation of the coincident agricultural, industrial and urban revolutions of the earlier century.

What degree of practice of the traditional Christian faith still remains? In place of the single nation-wide survey of 1851, we have, a century later, a mosaic of local surveys and national opinion polls which lend themselves to more than one interpretation. Some points, however, are clear. On any ordinary Sunday, only 10–15% of the adult population attend church, though probably 25% or more attend a service sometime during the year. Of the *rites de passage*, death is almost without exception given a religious celebration. Birth is followed by baptism in about 90% of cases, and religious marriages account for about 66% of the total. Somewhat under half of those baptised into the Church of England go on to be confirmed, and about a quarter of those confirmed recognise their membership, at least to the extent of taking Easter communion. The number of those who claim no religious affiliation seems to vary from survey to survey; this may be due in some part to local differences, but probably in greater part to the wording and presentation of the question on this subject. Thus the percentage of the population reported as 'religiously uncommitted' or having 'no religious affiliation' in the surveys compiled by Leslie Paul[4] varies from a low figure of 0·4% to a high point of 47·5%. Clearly there is no comparability here; what these variations show up is the large numbers of people having tenuous links with a church and the small number who have openly rejected all religious ties.

We have already seen that sect membership comprises only about 5% of the population. The Catholics and Nonconformists each represent between 10 and 20% of the population, leaving the Anglicans with about 60%. It is very difficult to be more precise than this, because of the different ways in which membership is recorded in each denomination. It is obvious that the Nonconformists have dropped back from their position of near equality with the Anglicans at the end of the nineteenth century; and equally obvious that the Catholics have advanced numerically, largely because of Irish immigration and higher fertility. There are some signs that the decline in religious participation has now stopped. It is argued that, since it has gone so far that mere social conformism can no longer be playing a positive role, there now stands revealed a measure of those truly committed to the Christian religion. This may be true for English Nonconformity and Anglicanism; it is less true for Irish Catholics in England, and for Nonconformists in Wales, where religious practice is an aspect of membership of a community, rather than a separate role which can be given up without profound adjustments of other roles.

The sociology of Catholicism and Judaism in Britain during the last two hundred years is relatively unknown territory. If it could be explored, the results might throw some light on the hypotheses connecting the various phases of industrialisation with religious changes. Knowledge of the degrees of lapsing and loyalty of the

Irish Catholics in English industrial towns should throw some light on the possible correlation between degree of social disorganisation and decay of religious practice, since these immigrants faced a greater cultural shock, and moved into lower positions in the socio-economic hierarchy, than did native Catholics or Protestants. Lenski's survey in Detroit showed a higher rate of practice among Catholics of the second and third immigrant generation than among those of the first. Did something comparable to this occur in England and Scotland? Or did the Catholic Church retain its hold on the Irish in England right from the beginning, because national loyalties resisted the disorganising effect of slum life, under-employment and the like? Whatever the position of Catholic immigrants and their descendants in the nineteenth century, it appears in the twentieth that the Catholic Church in Britain has found it easier than the Protestant denominations to maintain a high level of religious practice. At the very least, the church has not suffered massive defections of the faithful as in France and Italy. This raises the question as to whether there are some qualities of Catholic Christianity which, in the absence of unfavourable circumstances such as the strong association of Catholicism with bourgeois or aristocratic privileges, enable it to resist the erosion suffered by Protestant groups. One such quality may be the centralised hierarchical system which prescribes a definite and easy role for the layman; he does not have to help to build a congregation and to take responsibility for running it, as Nonconformist churches tend to require. Since the priests, i.e., the professionals, are in charge, adaptation to circumstances, and the adopting of new means, can be quicker than in organisations which tend to rely on congregational democracy in theory, and the devotion of an oligarchic minority in practice. (One is reminded of the differences between the thrusting chain-store and the cooperative.) This organisational aspect of the Catholic Church is connected with its theological principles. These require that men should believe in the saving power of Christ and receive his sacraments; they do not demand that people should 'feel better' for having gone to church. Neither do they demand that the church should be the basis for extensive moral crusades against alcohol or poverty, or war. Nonconformist Protestanism has always stressed the conversion experience and the subsequent efforts at Christian perfection; in organisation it has always stressed fellowship as both the means to, and the expression of, Christian charity. To construct or maintain groups in which a high emotional level of comradeship is attained is, in modern English society, extremely difficult, yet the expectation of this is embedded in the tradition. Disappointment with the actuality may lead to abandonment of the faith, in a way unknown to Catholicism with its different, and in a sense lower, expectations. It is of course true that Anglicanism has basically the same theology and organisation as Catholicism, yet has not maintained its hold to the same degree as the latter. But its historical association with political and economic privilege has disabled it from doing so, in the same way that continental Catholicism has been enfeebled by past privilege.

If we think of Christian religious ritual as a dramatic expression of the dependence of men on a moral power in the universe, then the Catholic play is written in every detail, and the main parts taken by word-perfect professional actors; it is easy for the layman to identify with the actors, even though he remains in the audience. The Nonconformist play is one for which the professionals provide only a bare outline, the laymen have to help to write and act. This is a harder task, particularly if those thrown together to do the job have never seen one another before, and may not do so again. The necessary community basis for success in the enterprise has been provided twice, by two different sets of circumstances. In the first, by the shared feeling of being saved from sin and demoralisation, and set apart from the wicked world; in the second, by having a similar social status of middle-class respectability, achieved and maintained by individual effort in the framework of a liberal-democratic state. Modern urban and suburban living does not provide any such favourable background.

It is of course a further question as to the social factors which influence the intensity of men's beliefs in God, and therefore their desire to join in some dramatic representation of his saving power. Clearly, in modern society, many feel no such desire. My point here is that where they do, they are more likely, given the social history of the different branches of Christianity in England, to satisfy that need in the Catholic rather than in the Protestant churches. One further point may be made here; the greater use of music, poetic language and the visual arts in Catholicism may help modern men to accept the basic creed of Christianity less critically than when it is embodied in a plain unvarnished statement in the vernacular. Rich symbolism allows many interpretations (that it permits superstitious ones has always been the ground of criticism of Catholicism by Protestants). Aesthetic satisfactions may silence intellectual uncertainties.

The future of Judaism in Western industrial societies is also of great sociological interest. Like the Irish in England and Scotland, the Jews in countries like England and the USA have experienced the cultural shock of immigrant status, and have reduced it by residential congregation and occupational specialisation. But the kind of occupational specialisation has been very different. They have arrived as self-employed artisans and traders, and have spread out into industry, commerce and the professions as self-employed or as employers. Thus they have, more than any other religious group, been affected by the urban way of living which is characteristic of Western industrial society, yet less than any other religious group, except possibly the French Protestants, by the fact of proletarian status. Since it is possible that urban life and wage-earning status each has its own specific influence on religious practice, the Jewish experience should be important, even though the numbers involved are small. The first thing to notice is that Judaism had become adapted to an urban way of life over many centuries, so that in some ways it fitted into its new surroundings, strange though they were in point of language and culture. The same sort of economic opportunities were there, and religious attitudes and practices did not inhibit the immigrants from seizing them. Yet these opportunities were shared among all groups in a *laissez-faire* type of economy, and there was no special status for Jews giving either privilege or disability. Thus the opportunities for mixing with non-Jews and assimilating to their ways of living were increased in the new countries.

We can see in eighteenth-century Britain that the Jews settled in England since 1657 began to be infected by the deism and rationalism of the Enlightenment in the same way as Anglicanism and old Dissent. The trickle of conversion to Anglicanism among richer Jewish families, and intermarriage at that level into Anglican families, bears witness to the beginnings of assimilation, which could only occur if there were a weakening of traditional religion. How far this might have gone if no further immigration occurred is impossible to estimate; the big immigrations of the late nineteenth century into Britain set a different norm of Jewish life, in which numbers and traditional congregation encouraged a perpetuation of the total immigrant culture, including religion. But the process of upward social mobility and educational assimilation has been very rapid, and has reproduced the opportunities of assimilation which the older-settled group confronted in the eighteenth and nineteenth centuries. Of course, the reproduction is not exact; it is now possible, without any social or legal disability resulting, for a

Jew to give up his own religious practice without adopting any form of Christianity. No definite step of apostasy and conversion is required; assimilation can be by easy stages, and need have no positive religious connotation. But the size of the Jewish middle-class community is now such that the range of non-Jewish contacts may be smaller, at least relatively, than in the earlier situation. Schooling up to university level may be segregated; suburban congregation is such that a full range of social activities can often be provided within each community. Nevertheless, the effect of middle-class urban living on British Jewry seems to be similar to its effect on Christian denominations; a low level of practice without a repudiation of the basic religious beliefs. The difference is that among Jewry the remaining poor Jews are more observant of their religion than their richer middle-class brethren, whereas among Christians there is still a slightly higher degree of religious practice among middle-class than among workers' families. It would seem that in escaping the experience of proletarianisation, Jewry ensured that whatever the strains and difficulties of adapting to the new industrial society, they would not result in the immediate widespread loss of traditional religious practices.

The positive response of a significant minority of industrial workers to Primitive Methodism and Calvinistic Baptism suggests that the change from peasant or farm labourer to industrial worker may effect a change rather than a destruction of religious practice. In this respect, it is worth recalling that the new associations of the nineteenth-century workers, their trade unions, friendly societies and cooperatives, all developed some ritual aspects, and all used religious language. For instance, the new rule book of the Ancient Order of Foresters in 1834 prescribed that prayers should be said at every meeting. The Chartists who advocated a general strike called it a 'Sacred Month'. Chartism produced its hymns, just as Wesleyanism did. (One might even argue that Chartism produced its irrational 'cargo cult' in the shape of land resettlement schemes as the way to a workers' commonwealth.) Only very gradually, and even now incompletely, prayers and hymns, uniforms and oaths, came to seem inappropriate in the Labour Movement. The extent to which membership in these new associations coincided with membership of the church and chapel is impossible to judge, but certainly the fast-growing friendly societies, who had two million members by 1850, must have included large numbers of the 'unchurched'. This has to be taken into account before we assess the effect of industrialisation on all forms of religion, not only on traditional forms of religious expression. It is understandable that Christian commentators living in the nineteenth century should take church attendance as their one significant measure; it is not so comprehensible that modern sociologists should accept this criterion from them.

An American study of the impact of textile factories on a hitherto purely agricultural district gives some insight into the specific effect of industrial employment on a peasant population, uncomplicated by those influences of long-distance migration and urbanism, which often occur in conjunction with the switch to factory employment. Liston Pope's *Millhands and Preachers*[5] is a vivid account of religious and occupational changes in a district of Carolina in which cotton textile mills were introduced on a large scale between 1890 and 1930. It culminates with an analysis of the religious and secular components of a wave of strikes in 1929 which attracted nation-wide attention. The mills were set up by local men with local capital, and employed only the local white population. Thus complications of race, and resentment of outsiders, did not enter into the picture. All the actors, except for some of the union organisers who appeared on the scene during the strikes, were local by birth, white and Protestant. The development of the mills increased the percentage of the population working in them from 3·5 to 27% between 1890 and 1930. Over the same period, the urban fraction of the population rose from 16 to 36%. Nevertheless, most of the mill workers lived in mill villages, dominated by the employers, rather than in towns. The class structure changed, with the middle-class 'uptown' population becoming somewhat larger and much richer, whilst the wages of the least skilled section of the mill workers were kept near subsistence level because of the constant influx of new workers from the always increasing population on the farms. The rate of population increases was such that, even with the opportunities of employment in the mills, and of emigration outside the district altogether, the average size of farm continued to decline, and the ratio of farm population to land to increase. The religious situation at the beginning of the period was a division of the population among Lutherans, Presbyterians, Methodists and Baptists, 36% of the population being church members.

Pope's first finding is that between 1890 to 1930 the overall level of religious affiliation dropped slightly, and then recovered to almost exactly the same level as existed in 1890. But whilst the mill workers showed a somewhat lower average level of membership, the expanded middle class showed a much higher level. The rural families barely changed their position. What was more striking than the small decline in religious membership among mill families was the different kind of group they patronised, and the impossibility of combining in one congregation mill and farm workers and 'uptown' families. The Lutherans and Presbyterians, who attempted such united congregations, failed, and lost all mill-family members. The Methodists and Baptists held their ground where they provided, often at the expense of the mill-owner, a separate church in which could take place the kind of services which suited the workers. These were services with less formality, more spontaneous lay participation, and more overt emotion. Also, the mill-people expected their church to be a community centre for the village. New sects, unheard-of in pre-industrial days, made their appearance, and although the leader usually arose from the farm population, he recruited effectively among the poorest mill families. These sects had a high birth and death rate, and often seemed to have no distinguishing mark one from the other, apart from the personality of the leader. Their services, even more than the adapted Methodist and Baptist ones, were of the 'holy-roller' emotional type. The better-established sects began to acquire some members from the less poor families, and these members might lead the sect into a more respectable and sober position. Then a new sect would find the field open for recruitment among the poorest. Pope could not trace any effect of sect-membership in raising the social status of a whole group of erstwhile poor workers. He did comment on the fact that whereas the denominations had conferences and committees which gave at least some attention to the social problems of the textile industry, such as child labour and low wages, the sects were concerned only with personal moral questions, such as sabbath observance, prohibition, mixed swimming pools, and style of dress. Nevertheless, the employers were more suspicious of the sectarian groups, which were independent of their patronage and roused their members to greater financial and other efforts for their churches. In fact, the poorest folk tended to polarise into those alienated from religion and those very fervent in their religious practices. (This is not to imply that the membership in each group was stable; it is typical of revivalist kinds of Christianity that there is a large turnover of members.) In the middle class, the non-religious group hardly existed, but the group of enthusiasts was also small.

The strikes of 1929 were sudden and violent. Union organisation came with the strikes rather than before it. The organisers, who frequently were atheistic outsiders, had to accept a kind of union meeting in which hymns and prayers played a large part. God was invoked by the workers, but he was equally freely invoked by those who took the employers' side, particularly by most of the professional ministers of religion. The division of the workers into those who were and those who were not religious did not prevent a unified organisation during the dispute.

It would be interesting to know if this episode could be matched in the periods of early factory organisation of an industry in Britain. The sudden switch from religious support of the old values of self-discipline and humility to religious sanction of radical strike action may well be typical of the early adaptation of workers to industrial occupations, wherever the scale of migration or of new settlements is not so great as to engender widespread loss of religious affiliation altogether. Pope's millhands and preachers have affinities with some of Hobsbawm's Catholic peasant rebels, where a religion sanctifying a hierarchic society is suddenly adapted to justify rebellion against that society.

There are three further points which throw light on the more general concerns of the sociology of religion. Pope shows that the emergent industrial bourgeoisie became more religious than its predecessors. This effect of industrialisation in increasing religious practice among the upper classes can be traced in France and England, where nineteenth-century devoutness replaced eighteenth-century scepticism, among Catholics in the one case and Protestants in the other. The functional argument from supposed human needs lays great stress on men having recourse to religion at times when ill-fortune and disaster strike, and worldly values seem meaningless. This accords with the position in which the upper classes have a merely formal religion, and the lower classes are more devout; such a situation may have been broadly true of pre-industrial France and Britain. But it is more difficult to reconcile with the growing religious practice of an industrial, as against a commercial or land-owning, upper class, or with the large-scale loss of religious practice during rapid urbanisation and factory organisation by the hard-hit proletariat of both these countries. It is also more difficult to reconcile with the fact of alienation from religion among the poorest, which can be seen on only a small scale in Pope's mill villages, but to a larger extent in the big industrial towns. It would seem that, just where the need for reassurance against anomie and frustration was the greatest, the religious response was least.

Finally the story of the strikes provides a comment on the assertion that one of the functions of religion is to hold a society together by reinforcing a common set of values. Certainly difference of religion did not provoke the industrial conflict, but as certainly it was powerless to prevent or heal it. Religious differentiation developed as class and occupational differences widened, and when an economic dispute arose religion sanctioned the values of each side to the dispute, not a common set of values. In fact cooperation between practising and non-practising Christians on the workers' side was easier to achieve than cooperation between practising Christian employers and practising Christian workers, in solving the dispute.

The great contrast of Britain and the USA in respect of current religious practice provides further evidence that the religious effects of industrialisation are not uniform, nor uniformly destructive. Both countries are highly industrialised, yet present a great contrast in their levels of religious practice and affiliation. The gap between high practice in the USA and low practice in Britain has certainly widened in the last fifty years, probably by growth in America as well as by decline in Britain. It cannot be attributed to the higher proportion of Catholics in America, for in that country the Protestants as well as the Catholics have increased their numbers faster than the population as a whole. Whilst there has been much controversy over the accuracy of American religious statistics, there is no question but that they represent a level of practice much higher than exists in Britain. Three features of American society, absent in Britain, have been invoked to explain the difference: the lack of any established church in America since independence; the effects of large-scale immigration from many parts of Europe; and the high valuation of equality of opportunity. Bryan Wilson, in his *Religion in Secular Society*,[6] stresses all these features. He accepts Herberg's argument that, a few small sects apart, all religious groups in the USA worship the same 'American way of life'; being American includes being religious, and finding in religion a sanction for the American values of individualism, activism, efficiency and self-improvement. The reasons why Americans give a religious expression to these values are two. First, the revived loyalties of Americans of the third and later immigrant generations to the faiths of their forefathers. Second, the need of all Americans for membership in a community offering warm personal relationships, a need arising in reaction against the vast, impersonal, ever-changing society in which they all perforce live. The need for identity and community is met through groups smaller than the vastness of America, hence the revival of attachment to churches which are still partly ethnic in character, and the persistence of Protestant attachment to a particular denomination.

Since all these groups have always had freedom and equal legal status, there is no reason for irreligion to grow as a means of protest against religious privilege; in this lies the first big difference from England where the Anglican Church is established by the state. Neither is there any reason why religious and social protest should be linked together in America, whereas in England the establishment of Anglicanism made the church seem a protector of all kinds of privilege. The variety of American religion is more apparent than real; if religion is to express the new-found unity of the nation, little diversity can be permitted. All must preach the moral values of Americanism; all must play down theological and other differences. The characteristic attitude was expressed perfectly by President Eisenhower when he said that a man should have a faith, no matter which it was. Since America was in fact as well as in dreams the land of freedom and opportunity for the many, even sects that in their beginning drew members from the poorest sections of the community began to preach the standard American values, as their members felt and approved the operation of these in their own lives. Wilson also endorses Herberg's further contention that since all religions are in fact preaching secular values, and organising 'synthetic' rather than 'real' communities, all are to a large degree secularised in spite of themselves. In America there is secularisation within the churches; in England there is secularisation by withdrawal from the churches, with the members who remain being 'truly' religious.

Let us look more carefully at this account of the American situation and its comparison with Britain. First of all, it must be recognised that Herberg's view of the three-generation process among immigrants, from high religious practice to low, and then back again in the third generation, is not well founded. It appears much more likely that the first-generation immigrants had the lowest rates of practice, whilst their children and grandchildren have shown continuously increasing rates. Lenski's careful studies in Detroit in the 1950s show this pattern for Catholics and for white Protestants.[7] A rather similar pattern emerges for white and Negro Protestants moving within the USA from country to expanding town. The actual migrants tend to lose touch with their churches; their children and grandchildren tend to regain it, or possibly to become affiliated to a new church. This overall rise in practice is connected with the rise in socio-economic status through the generations, for the better educated and better off in each religious group have higher rates of practice. Yet the actual duration of settlement in America, or in urban America, also seems to have an independent effect. The one religious group that, from Lenski's and other evidence, does not follow this pattern of increasing religious practice is American Jewry. Yet even in this group Herberg's view is not confirmed, for in each succeeding generation the level of practice is lower, a reversal of the Catholic and Protestant trends. It appears that Herberg generalised too widely from the appearance, among second-generation Jewish immigrants, of a number of articulate atheists and radicals, and from the subsequent diminution of this group. But this secularisation of a minority of a minority group does not much affect the overall picture. The apparent peculiarity of the trend of religious practice in American Jewry may be elucidated by relating it to the experience of a small upper-class white Protestant group, the Episcopalians. The social composition of this group is even more biased to the middle- and upper-socio-economic levels than that of the Jews, and both groups show equally low rates of regular religious practice, and yet clearly retain their religious and social identity.

The other point at which Herberg's evidence is open to challenge is his assertion that different groups in fact proclaim a common faith and share the same attitudes. Lenski's survey shows that, on the contrary, religious affiliation correlates with differences in political and social opinions, even when social-class differences are eliminated. Here Herberg relies perhaps too much on generalising from recent Protestant history, when general theological modernism, and the end of frontier-type religion, have helped to lower the barriers between different brands of Protestantism. His emphasis on similarity asserts oddly with the enormous and successful efforts of American Catholics to establish their own educational system, and with the widespread network of Jewish religious education and of Zionist activities. These all seem to endorse separate rather than common values. No doubt he is right in saying that as an urban middle-class standard of living spreads throughout American society, and as the linguistic and cultural differences associated with immigration disappear, all American religious groups have more common elements than in previous generations. But that they have become stronger *because* they have come to resemble one another so much that they are all, indifferently, vehicles of American patriotism is another and unsubstantiated proposition. If transposed to the British context it would mean that in our own more homogeneous society religion ought to be all the stronger, whereas the starting-point of the discussion is that this is patently not the case. The difficulty arises, I think, from Herberg moving from the factual statement that American society has changed from great heterogeneity towards homogeneity, to the statement of opinion that American society 'needed' to overcome the divisiveness of the period of rapid immigration and frontier expansion, and met this 'need' by infusing all religions with common American values. No doubt, American society would have moved even more smoothly to assimilation if the Protestant 'Know Nothings' hadn't harried the Irish Catholics in the mid-nineteenth century, but this 'need' didn't weaken the antipathy of the Protestants. How pathetically ineffective in unifying a society a supposedly common set of religious values can be is surely demonstrated by the failure of a common Protestant allegiance to achieve the assimilation of the white and black practitioners of that faith in America and Britain.

A similar questionable invocation of 'need' occurs in Wilson's discussion of denominational differences in the USA and Britain. He shows that denominations initially reflected cleavages in society, or sometimes produced them, as when Catholic, Lutheran and Jewish groups were added to the older Protestant communities of America. He then shows how in both countries the social base of these denominations has been eroded, as their respective societies have become more homogeneous. But, he argues, the British denominations have retained their distinctiveness; the American have not, but have all alike become suitable means for celebrating Americanism. He puts forward as a reason for this difference that British denominations have been under 'less pressure from the wider society', because whereas immigrant divisiveness threatened American unity, religious dissensions didn't threaten British social order. I find it very difficult to accept the view that when a society is more seriously threatened by divisiveness it is better able to provide a religious cure for this trouble, and I would think that human history would wear a more peaceful aspect if this were so. Again, we seem to be in the presence of a beneficent 'hidden hand' of functionalism, whereby a need of society is met by a religious change. The facts can be better interpreted, without invoking such mysterious needs, by reference to the social histories of the two countries.

The same difficulty arises over the individual's 'need' for community in an impersonal society. Wilson's acceptance of Herberg's thesis here involves him in saying that the British do not 'need' to create or maintain religious communities because they have not so completely destroyed local and class communities as the Americans have. But quite certainly the trend in Britain has been in the last few decades towards the destruction of the old communities, whilst the trend in religious practice has been continually downwards. If religious adherence reflected community membership this would be explicable, but if there is a 'need' which must be met by religion if other structures cannot meet it, then surely Britain ought to be experiencing a religious revival.

Finally, when they contend that in America the common moral values of the three big religious groups are in fact secular values, and therefore that the religions are secularised, Wilson and Herberg are playing a confusing trick with language. If the Judæo–Christian God is invoked to sanction economic individualism, suburban neighbourliness, and anti-communism, then in normal usage these values are religious, even if worldly. Most of the world's religions most of the time have been concerned with worldly though not necessarily amoral values, such as good health, prosperity, victory in war, justice and order in the group. Provided the believer connects these worldly values with a divine power who is looked up to as the sanction or protector of them, and whose relation to mankind requires ritual celebration, they should surely be recognised as religious values. By this trick of language, the problem at issue, why values should have a religious celebration in one country and not in the other, is apparently solved, but in fact left unanswered.

In both writers there seems to be an unresolved conflict between teleological arguments based on the 'needs' of societies and individuals, and causal arguments that religion is the dependent variable reflecting social values, social structures and social change.

MacIntyre in *Secularisation and Moral Change*[8] puts forward a rather different argument to explain the different scale of religious activity in industrial Britain and America. The consistent standpoint of his book is that moral change derives from changes in social structures and experience, and precedes religious change. In his view the loss of the greater part of the British proletariat to the church was due to their rejection of the old paternalistic view of society after their experience of life in the big industrial towns. But the incompleteness of their rejection of Christianity was due to the fact that in the nineteenth century there did emerge a visible class society in which some common interests, at least in maintaining the rules of the game, did develop, and some freedom of action was allowed to all the contending parties. This sort of society, in which the old values of hierarchy and paternalism gave way partially and gradually to new ones of tolerance and equality and compromise, has permitted a 'vestigial Christianity' to persist, but a Christianity which no longer enshrines a positive and coherent social ethic. The industrial revolution in Britain broke up a long-established class society, and constructed a looser and more impersonal variant of it. The values developing through experience in that society are not those of whole-hearted paternalism and ascription of status, nor those of whole-hearted belief in equality of opportunity, nor yet those of whole-hearted egalitarian socialism; they are the 'secondary virtues', the value of fair play and mutual toleration of different interests. In America, the industrial revolution occurred in an initially more egalitarian society, holding strongly to the values of personal liberty and equality of opportunity. The progress of industrialisation, as it swept upwards successive waves of immigrants, confirmed these values. Religion is stronger there because there is a unity of positive values; they are effectively espoused by all of the superficially differing groups. 'The difference between the secularisation of English society consequent on industrialisation, and the lack of secularisation in American society is in the end the product of two different class structures, one of which allows for there being a national community of values and the other of which allows that national community of values to exist at the level of what I call the secondary virtues.'[9] 'The industrial revolution in America was, and in England was not, contained within the pre-existing value system.'[10]

This analysis I find more coherent than Wilson's, though it points to further unanswered questions. Since all European industrial revolutions have been similar to England's and different from America's in respect of causing a break-up of an established hierarchic social structure, it would seem that other things being equal all should show similar religious results to the English. But in fact the level of adherence and practice, or withdrawal from, or active hostility to, religion, is very variable in the different European states. Some of these differences are explicable in terms of national sentiments, some in terms of the majority or minority positions of a particular faith. Others are hard to explain except in terms of social inertia, e.g., the centuries-old abstention from Catholic practice in some parts of France. It would seem that social-class influences on morals, values and religious attitudes are not the only ones that have to be taken into account.

Our second question concerns the relative openness of Catholicism and Protestantism to the weakening influences of industrial society. I have already argued that in its British setting Catholicism has been more resistant than Anglicanism or Nonconformity. (Sectarian Christianity also probably retains its very limited strength, though individual sects have a precarious life.) Does it follow that other Protestant populations have lost the habit of religion more than their

Catholic counterparts? The difficulties of accurate comparison of statistics of membership and practice are great, as between two traditions which lay such different stress on weekly church attendance, but the position is broadly as follows. The lowest rates of church attendance are to be found in the almost exclusively Protestant countries of Norway and Sweden. There is an urban-rural differential, the big towns showing the lowest levels; nevertheless, rural levels are also very low, so that these countries, which are not the most heavily industrialised or urbanised in Europe, show the least religious participation. Protestant England shows rather higher rates of attendance, Scotland and Wales higher again; but the Catholics in these countries score considerably higher. The same sort of ratio between Protestants and Catholics can be seen in the USA, although the absolute levels are higher. The USA statistics also show the variation among different Protestant denominations, with the Lutherans showing rates of regular practice almost as high as the Catholics.

In Western Germany, the rates of both Catholic and Protestant practice are similar to the American, the Catholics still showing the higher rate. But the distribution of the population claiming no religious affiliation suggests that this group is composed more of lapsed Protestants than lapsed Catholics. In Holland, the same phenomenon can be traced, those owning no religious affiliation are predominantly lapsed Protestants or the descendants thereof. Practice is very high among Dutch Catholics, much lower among the members of the old Reformed Church, in a middle position among the 10% of the population in the neo-Calvinist New Reformed Church.

In France, the Protestant minority retains its strength, whilst Catholic practice is on average much lower. Belgium and Italy, almost purely Catholic countries, show similar average rates to the French, i.e., about 40% of nominal Catholics practising, but in France at least there is a significant proportion owning no religious affiliation (15 to 20% in different localities, compared with 3% in Western Germany and 17% in Holland).[11]

Overall national or even regional figures conceal . important differences in religious practice, and in the local incidence of urbanism and industrialisation. We have noted that rural Sweden and Norway have very low rates of practice; it is also clear that some of the lowest levels of Catholic practice can be found in rural France, and that this low level antedates the general development of industrialisation in the whole country. It is certainly obvious that neither urbanism nor industry bears the sole responsibility for an almost complete loss of religious practice, whether in a Catholic or a Protestant setting.

It is probable that in some contexts the devotion of Protestants is heightened when they are in a minority position. Michael Fogarty, after a survey of data available in the 1950s for Western European countries, concludes that the 'figures suggest (rather than prove) that the proportion of active members of the Protestant churches tends to equal or exceed that of the Catholic Church where Protestantism is a minority, but to fall short where it is dominant.'[12]

1. K. Morioka, 'Contemporary Changes in Japanese Religion', in N. Birnbaum and G. Lenzer, *Sociology and Religion*, 1969.

2. For a detailed analysis of the 1851 Census, see W. Pickering, 'The 1851 Religious Census—a useless experiment?', *British Journal of Sociology*, vol. XVIII, 1967.

3. J. Bossy, 'More Northumbrian Congregations', *Recusant History*, vol. X, 1969.

4. L. Paul, *The Payment and Deployment of the Clergy*, 1964.

5. L. Pope, *Millhands and Preachers*, 1942.

6. B. Wilson, *Religion in Secular Society*, 1966.

7. G. Lenski, *The Religious Factor*, 1961.

8. A. MacIntyre, *Secularisation and Moral Change*, 1967.

9. ibid., p. 34.

10. ibid., p. 34.

11. All figures are drawn from M. P. Fogarty, *Christian Democracy in Western Europe, 1820–1953*, 1957, ch. XXII.

12. ibid.

BIBLIOGRAPHY

The titles here listed are all additional to those referred to in the text. Even so, the list is clearly selective rather than inclusive. I have given preference to empirical studies bearing on the theoretical questions and hypotheses discussed in the text, since I believe that early acquaintance with the raw material of the sociology of religion helps the student to grasp the theoretical questions at issue. In choosing books concerned with a particular religious tradition, I have preferred, where possible, those written by a believer or participant in that tradition.

Finally I have indicated, in the titles relevant to Chapter 1, classics by Hume, Bergson, William James and Otto which fill gaps in my own brief treatment of the history of thought in the sociology of religion.

The dates refer to the first publication of the book, or, in the case of translations, the first publication of the English translation.

CHAPTER 1

H. Becker, 'Sacred and Secular Societies'; essay in *Through Values to Social Interpretation*, Durham, USA 1950

H. Bergson, *Two Sources of Morality and Religion*, London 1935

N. Birnbaum and G. Lenzer (Eds.), *Sociology of Religion*, Englewood Cliffs, USA 1969

H. Carrier, *Sociology of Religious Belonging*, New York 1965

M. Eliade, *Patterns in Comparative Religion*, London 1958

D. Hume, 'Natural History of Religion'; essay in *Essays Moral, Political and Literary*, London 1770

W. James, *Varieties of Religious Experience*, London 1912

R. Otto, *The Holy*, London 1926

R. Robertson (Ed.), *Sociology of Religion;* selected readings, Harmonds-
    worth 1970

CHAPTER 2

A. J. Arberry (Ed.), *Religion in the Middle East*, Cambridge 1969

E. R. Bevan, *Christianity*, London 1933

M. Douglas, *Natural Symbols*, London 1970

I. Epstein, *Judaism*, London 1959

H. Frankfort, Mrs H. Frankfort, J. A. Wilson, T. Jacobsen, *Before
    Philosophy*, London 1949

C. Humphreys, *Buddhism*, London 1962

J. Kitagawa, *Religion in Japanese History*, New York 1966

G. C. Pande, *Studies in the Origins of Buddhism*, Allahabad, 1957

F. Rahman, *Islam*, London 1966

K. M. Sen, *Hinduism*, Harmondsworth 1961

D. H. Smith, *Chinese Religions*, London 1968

H. R. Trevor-Roper, *Rise of Christian Europe*, London 1965

J. S. Trimingham, *The Influence of Islam upon Africa*, London 1968

C. K. Yang, *Religion in Chinese Society*, California 1961

CHAPTER 3

M. Banton (Ed.), *Anthropological Approaches to the Study of Religion*,
    London 1966

W. J. Goode, *Religion Among the Primitives*, Glencoe, USA 1951

V. Lanternari, *Religions of the Oppressed*, London 1963

C. Lévi-Strauss, *Structural Anthropology*, London 1968

G. Parrinder, *Witchcraft: African and European*, London 1958

G. Parrinder, *Religion in Africa*, Harmondsworth 1969

R. Redfield, *The Primitive World and its Transformations*, Cornell 1953

M. Srinivas, 'Sanskritization and Westernization'; from N. Birnbaum and
    G. Lenzer (Eds.), *Sociology of Religion*, Prentice-Hall 1969

CHAPTER 4

P. Berger, *Sacred Canopy*, New York 1967

P. Berger, *Rumour of Angels*, New York 1969

S. Freud, *Civilisation and its Discontents*, London 1930
T. Parsons, *Structure of Social Action*, Chapter XVII, New York 1937
T. Parsons, *Essays in Sociological Theory*, Chapter VI, Glencoe, USA 1949
R. Robertson, *The Sociological Interpretation of Religion*, Oxford 1970

CHAPTER 5

F. C. Conybeare, *Russian Dissenters*, Cambridge, USA 1921
D. Coomer, *English Dissent*, London 1946
N. J. Demerath and P. E. Hammond, *Religion in Social Context*, New York 1969
D. A. Martin, *A Sociology of English Religion*, London 1967
S. Thrupp, *Millennial Dreams in Action*, The Hague 1962

CHAPTER 6

Journal of Comparative Studies in Society and History, The Hague 1958: Articles by R. Coulborn, 'State and Religion: Iran, India, China', and J. Strayer, 'State and Religion'
A. H. M. Jones, *Decline of the Ancient World*, London 1966
M. Loewe, *Imperial China*, London 1966
H. N. Sinha, *The Development of Indian Polity*, New York 1963
D. E. Smith, *India as a Secular State*, Princeton, USA 1963
T. R. Ware, *The Orthodox Church*, Harmondsworth 1963

CHAPTER 7

M. J. Kitch (Ed.), *Capitalism and the Reformation*, London 1967
H. R. Trevor-Roper, *Religious Reformation and Social Change*, London 1967

CHAPTER 8

F. Boulard, *Introduction to Religious Sociology*, London 1960
S. Burgalassi, *Italiani in Chiesa*, Brescia 1967
M. Hayward and W. C. Fletcher (Eds.), *Religion in the Soviet State*, London 1969
F. Houtart and E. Pin, *The Church and the Latin-American Revolution*, New York 1965

K. Inglis, *Churches and the Working Classes in Victorian England*, London 1963

F. A. Isambert, *Christianisme et Classe Ouvrière*, Paris 1961

K. Morioka and W. H. Newell (Eds.), *Sociology of Japanese Religion*, Leiden 1968

INDEX

71 72 73 74   12 11 10 9 8 7 6 5 4 3 2 1

haRpeR ☙ ɕoRchbooĸs

American Studies: General

CARL N. DEGLER: Out of Our Past: *The Forces that Shaped Modern America* CN/2

ROBERT L. HEILBRONER: The Limits of American Capitalism TB/1305

JOHN HIGHAM, Ed.: The Reconstruction of American History TB/1068

JOHN F. KENNEDY: A Nation of Immigrants. *Illus. Revised and Enlarged. Introduction by Robert F. Kennedy* TB/1118

GUNNAR MYRDAL: An American Dilemma: *The Negro Problem and Modern Democracy. Introduction by the Author.*
Vol. I TB/1443; Vol. II TB/1444

GILBERT OSOFSKY, Ed.: The Burden of Race: *A Documentary History of Negro-White Relations in America* TB/1405

ARNOLD ROSE: The Negro in America: *The Condensed Version of Gunnar Mydral's An American Dilemma* TB/3048

American Studies: Colonial

BERNARD BAILYN: The New England Merchants in the Seventeenth Century TB/1149

ROBERT E. BROWN: Middle-Class Democracy and Revolution in Massachusetts, 1691–1780. *New Introduction by Author* TB/1413

JOSEPH CHARLES: The Origins of the American Party System TB/1049

American Studies: The Revolution to 1900

GEORGE M. FREDRICKSON: The Inner Civil War: *Northern Intellectuals and the Crisis of the Union* TB/1358

WILLIAM W. FREEHLING: Prelude to Civil War: *The Nullification Controversy in South Carolina, 1816-1836* TB/1359

HELEN HUNT JACKSON: A Century of Dishonor: *The Early Crusade for Indian Reform.* ‡ *Edited by Andrew F. Rolle* TB/3063

RICHARD B. MORRIS, Ed.: Alexander Hamilton and the Founding of the Nation. *New Introduction by the Editor* TB/1448

RICHARD B. MORRIS: The American Revolution Reconsidered TB/1363

GILBERT OSOFSKY, Ed.: Puttin' On Ole Massa: *The Slave Narratives of Henry Bibb, William Wells Brown, and Solomon Northup* ‡ TB/1432

American Studies: The Twentieth Century

WILLIAM E. LEUCHTENBURG: Franklin D. Roosevelt and the New Deal: 1932-1940. † *Illus.* TB/3025

WILLIAM E. LEUCHTENBURG, Ed.: The New Deal: *A Documentary History* + HR/1354

Asian Studies

WOLFGANG FRANKE: China and the West: *The Cultural Encounter, 13th to 20th Centuries. Trans. by R. A. Wilson* TB/1326

L. CARRINGTON GOODRICH: A Short History of the Chinese People. *Illus.* TB/3015

BENJAMIN I. SCHWARTZ: Chinese Communism and the Rise of Mao TB/1308

Economics & Economic History

PETER F. DRUCKER: The New Society: *The Anatomy of Industrial Order* TB/1082

ROBERT L. HEILBRONER: The Great Ascent: *The Struggle for Economic Development in Our Time* TB/3030

W. ARTHUR LEWIS: The Principles of Economic Planning. *New Introduction by the Author*° TB/1436

Historiography and History of Ideas

J. BRONOWSKI & BRUCE MAZLISH: The Western Intellectual Tradition: *From Leonardo to Hegel* TB/3001

WILHELM DILTHEY: Pattern and Meaning in History: *Thoughts on History and Society.*° *Edited with an Intro. by H. P. Rickman* TB/1075

J. H. HEXTER: More's Utopia: *The Biography of an Idea. Epilogue by the Author* TB/1195

ARTHUR O. LOVEJOY: The Great Chain of Being: *A Study of the History of an Idea* TB/1009

History: Medieval

F. L. GANSHOF: Feudalism TB/1058

DENYS HAY: The Medieval Centuries ° TB/1192

HENRY CHARLES LEA: A History of the Inquisition of the Middle Ages. || *Introduction by Walter Ullmann* TB/1456

---

† The New American Nation Series, edited by Henry Steele Commager and Richard B. Morris.
‡ American Perspectives series, edited by Bernard Wishy and William E. Leuchtenburg.
a History of Europe series, edited by J. H. Plumb.
§ The Library of Religion and Culture, edited by Benjamin Nelson.
|| Researches in the Social, Cultural, and Behavioral Sciences, edited by Benjamin Nelson.
≗ Harper Modern Science Series, edited by James R. Newman.
° Not for sale in Canada.
+ Documentary History of the United States series, edited by Richard B. Morris.
# Documentary History of Western Civilization series, edited by Eugene C. Black and Leonard W. Levy.
Λ The Economic History of the United States series, edited by Henry David et al.
¶ European Perspectives series, edited by Eugene C. Black.
** Contemporary Essays series, edited by Leonard W Levy.
* The Stratum Series, edited by John Hale.

History: Renaissance & Reformation

JACOB BURCKHARDT: The Civilization of the Renaissance in Italy. *Introduction by Benjamin Nelson and Charles Trinkaus. Illus.*
Vol. I TB/40; Vol. II TB/41

JOEL HURSTFIELD: The Elizabethan Nation
TB/1312

ALFRED VON MARTIN: Sociology of the Renaissance. ° *Introduction by W. K. Ferguson*
TB/1099

J. H. PARRY: The Establishment of the European Hegemony: 1415-1715: *Trade and Exploration in the Age of the Renaissance* TB/1045

History: Modern European

MAX BELOFF: The Age of Absolutism, 1660-1815
TB/1062

ALAN BULLOCK: Hitler, A Study in Tyranny. ° *Revised Edition. Illus.* TB/1123

JOHANN GOTTLIEB FICHTE: Addresses to the German Nation. *Ed. with Intro. by George A. Kelly* ¶ TB/1366

H. STUART HUGHES: The Obstructed Path: *French Social Thought in the Years of Desperation* TB/1451

JOHAN HUIZINGA: Dutch Cviilization in the 17th Century and Other Essays TB/1453

JOHN MCMANNERS: European History, 1789-1914: *Men, Machines and Freedom* TB/1419

FRANZ NEUMANN: Behemoth: *The Structure and Practice of National Socialism, 1933-1944*
TB/1289

A. J. P. TAYLOR: From Napoleon to Lenin: *Historical Essays* ° TB/1268

H. R. TREVOR-ROPER: Historical Essays TB/1269

Philosophy

HENRI BERGSON: Time and Free Will: *An Essay on the Immediate Data of Consciousness* °
TB/1021

G. W. F. HEGEL: Phenomenology of Mind. ° ||
Introduction by George Lichtheim TB/1303

H. J. PATON: The Categorical Imperative: *A Study in Kant's Moral Philosophy* TB/1325

MICHAEL · POLANYI: Personal Knowledge: *Towards a Post-Critical Philosophy* TB/1158

LUDWIG WITTGENSTEIN: The Blue and Brown Books ° TB/1211

LUDWIG WITTGENSTEIN: Notebooks, 1914-1916
TB/1441

Political Science & Government

C. E. BLACK: The Dynamics of Modernization: *A Study in Comparative History* TB/1321

DENIS W. BROGAN: Politics in America. *New Introduction by the Author* TB/1469

KARL R. POPPER: The Open Society and Its Enemies *Vol. I: The Spell of Plato* TB/1101
Vol. II: The High Tide of Prophecy: Hegel, Marx, and the Aftermath TB/1102

CHARLES SCHOTTLAND, Ed.: The Welfare State **
TB/1323

JOSEPH A. SCHUMPETER: Capitalism, Socialism and Democracy TB/3008

PETER WOLL, Ed.: Public Administration and Policy: *Selected Essays* TB/1284

Psychology

LUDWIG BINSWANGER: Being-in-the-World: *Selected Papers.* || *Trans. with Intro. by Jacob Needleman* TB/1365

MIRCEA ELIADE: Cosmos and History: *The Myth of the Eternal Return* § TB/2050

SIGMUND FREUD: On Creativity and the Unconscious: *Papers on the Psychology of Art, Literature, Love, Religion.* § *Intro. by Benjamin Nelson* TB/45

J. GLENN GRAY: The Warriors: *Reflections on Men in Battle. Introduction by Hannah Arendt* TB/1294

WILLIAM JAMES: Psychology: *The Briefer Course. Edited with an Intro. by Gordon Allport* TB/1034

Religion

TOR ANDRAE: Mohammed: *The Man and his Faith* TB/62

KARL BARTH: Church Dogmatics: *A Selection. Intro. by H. Hollwitzer. Ed. by G. W. Bromiley* TB/95

NICOLAS BERDYAEV: The Destiny of Man TB/61

MARTIN BUBER: The Prophetic Faith TB/73

MARTIN BUBER: Two Types of Faith: *Interpenetration of Judaism and Christianity*
TB/75

RUDOLF BULTMANN: History and Eschatalogy: *The Presence of Eternity* TB/91

EDWARD CONZE: Buddhism: *Its Essence and Development. Foreword by Arthur Waley*
TB/58

H. G. CREEL: Confucius and the Chinese Way
TB/63

FRANKLIN EDGERTON, Trans. & Ed.: The Bhagavad Gita TB/115

M. S. ENSLIN: Christian Beginnings TB/5

M. S. ENSLIN: The Literature of the Christian Movement TB/6

HENRI FRANKFORT: Ancient Egyptian Religion: *An Interpretation* TB/77

IMMANUEL KANT: Religion Within the Limits of Reason Alone. *Introduction by Theodore M. Greene and John Silber* TB/67

GABRIEL MARCEL: Homo Viator: *Introduction to a Metaphysic of Hope* TB/397

H. RICHARD NIEBUHR: Christ and Culture TB/3

H. RICHARD NIEBUHR: The Kingdom of God in America TB/49

SWAMI NIKHILANANDA, Trans. & Ed.: The Upanishads TB/114

F. SCHLEIERMACHER: The Christian Faith. *Introduction by Richard R. Niebuhr.*
Vol. I TB/108 Vol. II TB/109

Sociology and Anthropology

KENNETH B. CLARK: Dark Ghetto: *Dilemmas of Social Power. Foreword by Gunnar Myrdal*
TB/1317

KENNETH CLARK & JEANNETTE HOPKINS: A Relevant War Against Poverty: *A Study of Community Action Programs and Observable Social Change* TB/1480

GARY T. MARX: Protest and Prejudice: *A Study of Belief in the Black Community* TB/1435

ROBERT K. MERTON, LEONARD BROOM, LEONARD S. COTTRELL, JR., Editors: Sociology Today: *Problems and Prospects* ||
Vol. I TB/1173; Vol. II TB/1174

GILBERT OSOFSKY: Harlem: The Making of a Ghetto: *Negro New York, 1890-1930* TB/1381

PHILIP RIEFF: The Triumph of the Therapeutic: *Uses of Faith After Freud* TB/1360

GEORGE ROSEN: Madness in Society: *Chapters in the Historical Sociology of Mental Illness.* || *Preface by Benjamin Nelson* TB/1337